Wallace Library

DUE DATE (stamped in blue)
RETURN DATE (stamped in black)

American Independence through Prussian Eyes

FREDERICK THE GREAT IN 1781

(From a painting by Anton Graff)

American Independence through Prussian Eyes

*A Neutral View of the Peace Negotiations
of 1782-1783: Selections from the Prussian
Diplomatic Correspondence*

Translated and Edited by

MARVIN L. BROWN, JR.

DUKE UNIVERSITY PRESS · Durham, North Carolina · 1959

Printed in the United States of America
by the Seeman Printery, Inc., Durham, N. C.

Preface

THE PURPOSE of the publication of these selections from the Prussian diplomatic correspondence, the central figure of which was Frederick the Great, is to present a neutral power's view of the negotiations for American independence. While American, British, French, Spanish, and Dutch material, reflecting the policies of the powers concerned, has been thoroughly studied in connection with the negotiations of 1782-1783, the viewpoint of this powerful neutral trying to peer into the negotiations has been neglected. P. L. Haworth's article, "Frederick the Great and the American Revolution," *American Historical Review*, IX (1904), traces Frederick's role during the early years of the war but does not deal with the negotiations of 1782-1783. A supplementary short study, J. G. Rosengarten, *Frederick the Great and the United States* (Lancaster, Pa., 1906), which incidentally gives attention to the legend that Frederick the Great gave Washington a sword, is not based on the correspondence collected here. A broader study, F. Kapp, *Friedrich der Grosse und die Vereinigten Staaten* (Leipzig, 1871), likewise cites none of this correspondence.

In a limited and restricted way the correspondence collected and translated here supplements the *Politische Correspondenz* of Frederick the Great, since that voluminous work reaches only to 30 March 1782, having been broken off by the death of its editor, Professor Gustav Bertold Volz. Material from five of Frederick's letters which are in that set appears here. To the best of my knowledge that is the only place where any portions of this correspondence are published. None of the letters are to be found in

Francis Wharton, *The Revolutionary Diplomatic Correspondence of the United States,* or in Jared Sparks, *The Diplomatic Correspondence of the American Revolution.* B. F. Stevens' set of remarkable reproductions, *Facsimiles of Manuscripts in European Archives Relating to America, 1773-1783,* does not include Prussian correspondence and contains only twenty-three documents of any kind for the years 1782-1783. The very extensive transcripts collected by George Bancroft from foreign archives on subjects related to American history, which are in the New York Public Library, include Austrian but not Prussian correspondence relative to negotiations for independence in 1782-1783. Besides an article by myself in *The Historian,* XVIII (1956), pp. 189-201, summarizing the substance of Prussian reaction to the negotiations for American independence, I have never seen any other citations of the following collection of documents.

The transcripts of the bulk of these letters I found in the National Archives, filed with a despatch of 1881, having been given to the United States by Germany at that time. These I have supplemented with material from the very extensive *Facsimiles from German Archives, Preussisches Geheimes Staatsarchiv, Berlin-Dahlem,* a photostatic collection in the Manuscripts Division of the Library of Congress which was made almost fifty years later. There are, however, portions of the 1881 transcripts which do not appear in the photostats. Since the 1881 transcripts begin with 24 June 1782, none of them are to be found in Volz's collection.

I have made the following translations for the benefit of the general reader and for the student who does not yet read French easily. Therefore my principal effort has been to give the most faithful rendition of the original text that would be easily understandable to readers of today.

My greatest indebtedness is to the Faculty Research and Professional Development Fund of North Carolina State College, through which a generous grant for a publication subsidy was made available to me.

I am grateful for various kinds of aid I have received. I am especially indebted to my wife, Elizabeth Winnifred Brown, who not only aided me by checking much of my translation but made the whole project pleasant work.

I am indebted to the staff of the Diplomatic and Judicial Records Branch of the National Archives and to the staff of the Manuscripts Division of the Library of Congress, both of whom were very helpful and patient. Like all who do any work in American diplomatic history, I am indebted to Professor Samuel Flagg Bemis, not only for his work in obtaining the photostatic collection in the Library of Congress but also for his *Diplomacy of the American Revolution,* which influenced my three introductory sections and explanatory notes. I am indebted to a number of librarians, particularly Mrs. Katherine A. Edsall of the D. H. Hill Library of North Carolina State College. I am also indebted to Professor Lynn M. Case of the University of Pennsylvania, whose thoroughness as a dissertation supervisor first caused me to go to the National Archives, in connection with Bismarck's European policies. As a result of this research I found most of the following documents. I wish to thank Professor Ernst Posner of the American University for valuable information about the *Preussisches Geheimes Staatsarchiv* and Prussian archivists, and I am also grateful to Professor Harold T. Parker of Duke University for criticisms of the manuscript. Finally, I want to express my gratitude for the courteous aid given me by Mr. Ashbel G. Brice and the staff of The Duke University Press.

M. L. B.

Raleigh, N. C.
November 2, 1957

Contents

Introduction xi

Source Note xvii

Negotiations before the News of the Defense of Gibraltar   3

The preliminary Treaties   77

Negotiations for the definitive Treaties   161

Epilogue   206

Index   207

Introduction

WHILE SEARCHING in the National Archives in Washington for American reaction to the several Bismarckian alliances, including the Alliance of the Three Emperors of 1881, the editor found an extraordinarily large enclosure sent with a despatch from Berlin dated 20 July 1881. Upon closer inspection the nearly four hundred pages turned out to be excerpts from the correspondence between Frederick the Great and his ambassadors in London and Paris relative to the question of American independence in the peace negotiations of 1782-1783.

On 2 March 1881 Secretary of State William M. Evarts wrote the following letter to the American minister in Berlin:

SIR:

In view of the preparations making in this country for celebration of the one-hundredth anniversary of peace and the recognition of American Independence, the President[1] deems the present a suitable time to begin the work of obtaining, so far as may be practicable, complete copies of all the correspondence in the archives of foreign governments, in any way bearing on the peace negotiations of 1783, in order that the same may be available for use, for historical purposes.

I have therefore to request you to bring the subject to the attention of the Imperial German Government, and to ask for permission to cause copies to be made of such unpublished papers and documents as may exist in the archives of the German Empire, at Berlin or elsewhere, relative to the peace negotiations in question, as the Imperial German Government may deem it proper to submit to the inspection of your legation for the purpose.

In addition to making this formal request of the German Imperial

[1] President Hayes had on this date one more day to serve.

Government, I will thank you to take measures to obtain such information as may be obtainable, as to documents relating to this subject which may exist in the M.S. collections of families, with a view of ultimately obtaining copies of such papers as may be of value.

I am, Sir,

W^m. M. EVARTS

This request was promptly made to the German Foreign Office, and on 19 May 1881 the American minister was sent this reply:

BERLIN, 19 May 1881

FOREIGN OFFICE

The undersigned has the honor of replying to the esteemed note of 17 March last, concerning the celebration of the one-hundredth anniversary of the Treaty of Versailles and the recognition of American Independence, to inform the Envoy Extraordinary and Minister Plenipotentiary of the United States of America, Mr. Andrew D. White, that the Royal Prussian Privy State Archives bearing upon these events contain certain copious and valuable material upon the institution of proceedings looking to peace with America, upon the relations between England and France, and the conclusion of the Treaty of Peace.

This matter contained in the French and English despatches has, after careful inspection of the political correspondence bearing upon the events referred to, been collected and indexed. The copying of the documents, which will occupy some time, has begun.

While expressing his purpose to transmit the copies when ready, the undersigned avails himself of this occasion to renew to the Envoy the assurances of his most distinguished consideration.

/signed/ LIMBURG-STIRUM[2]

On 19 July 1881 the material was sent to the legation. There were six packets of correspondence, sealed with the seal of the Prussian State Archives, including 208 pages of correspondence between King Frederick II and his ambassador in London, Count

---

[2] Count Limburg-Stirum was an important official under Bismarck in the foreign office; technically he was *Interimischer Leiter des auswärtigen Amtes*. The translation of his letter is the official one, to be found in the National Archives.

Lusi, in four of the packets, and 175 pages of the correspondence exchanged between Frederick and his ambassador in Paris, Baron von der Goltz, in the other two packets. This correspondence was arranged, for the most part, in a chronological sequence of instructions (*rescrits* and *ordres immediats*) and despatches, though one packet contained only instructions sent to Lusi.

To the best of my knowledge no use was made of these documents by the United States government. The celebration of the centennial of Yorktown, however, brought attention to German-American relations, dramatically emphasized by the invitation to seven descendants of von Steuben, the officer who was first notified of the proposed surrender. This invitation was accepted, and on 27 September 1881 the successor of White, H. Sidney Everett, reported that the Emperor William I was "delighted and touched by this evidence of the gratitude of the United States" and that it gave "great satisfaction" to Bismarck.

Who selected these documents is not altogether clear. The post records of the American legation in Berlin shed no light on the problem. Archivrat Friedlaender[3] certified the documents as being copies of those in the Prussian Archives. The letter of 19 May indicates the Prussian officials made the selections themselves, and Friedlaender's signature suggests at least his responsibility for the choice. Regardless of who did the work, a comparison of these papers with the photostatic *Facsimiles from German Archives, Preussisches Geheimes Staatsarchiv, Berlin-Dahlem* in the Manuscripts Division of the Library of Congress demonstrates

---

[3] According to information furnished by the *Bundesarchiv* at Cologne and by the *Deutsches Zentralarchiv* at Merseburg (Soviet Zone), which now holds the documents which were once in the Berlin-Dahlem archives, this official was Archivrat Ernst Friedlaender (1841-1903), son of the well-known archivist Archivrat Emil Gottlieb Friedlaender (1805-1878). Friedrich Kapp acknowledged the aid of an Archivrat Friedlaender in the preparation of his book, *Friedrich der Grosse und die Vereinigten Staaten* (Leipzig, 1871), but this must have been the father, because Ernst Friedlaender did not join the staff of the *Geheimes Staatsarchiv* until 1874. The archives in 1881 were under the direction of the historian Heinrich von Sybel.

that a somewhat more complete set of selections should have been made. In the first place, Frederick's correspondence with his minister plenipotentiary at The Hague, von Thulemeier, and with Count von Nostitz, who occupied the same post in Madrid, contains some material which should not have been overlooked. In the second place, the correspondence in the 1881 transcripts does not begin until 24 June 1782, although Franklin started negotiations with Oswald in April. In the third place, a number of significant letters written in the second half of 1782 and in 1783 are omitted. For these reasons the editor decided to supplement this correspondence with additional material from the photostats in the Library of Congress. The decision arbitrarily to begin with 1 January 1782 has the merit of picking up the thread well in advance of the first American negotiations in Paris, but has no particular significance from Frederick's point of view. The German transcripts of 1881 end with 30 June 1783. They are supplemented by the editor only to this point. Prussia seemed to regard the preliminary treaties as practically final, and primarily devoted its interest in America afterwards to questions of trade, even though the signing of the Prussian-American trade treaty was long delayed.

In the 1881 copies of the instructions to Count Lusi in London, found in the National Archives, there appear thirty-three letters from Frederick which were not reproduced in the Library of Congress photostats. The reason for the absence of this group of letters from the photostats, which were made in the late 1920's, cannot be explained by the editor. The 1881 transcripts also include a long letter about British policy written by Grantham to Stepney in Berlin and given to Frederick and a further summary of British diplomacy which do not appear in the photostats. These thirty-five items, found only in the 1881 transcripts, have been indicated in the following translated texts by a †. Additional letters not sent as part of the 1881 selections but appearing in the Library of Congress photostats are indicated by asterisks. Selections found in both of these overlapping sources are printed without any special designation. The 1881 German transcripts are the basis of this collection, and all of them are included. While these criticisms may be made of the 1881 selection of documents, there would seem to have been no deliberate avoidance of material.

Both sources of the correspondence collected here have their limitations, since they are made up almost exclusively of the exchange of instructions and despatches between Frederick and his ministers. The editor has been unable to consult these in the original or other material in the *Preussisches Geheimes Staatsarchiv* in Berlin-Dahlem, because, unfortunately, these archives are in the Soviet Zone of Germany.

For the most part the following selections are portions of long despatches, usually covering a number of subjects, rather than complete letters. This applies both in the case of the selections made in 1881 by the Germans and in the case of the supplementary selections from the Library of Congress photostats made by the editor. Since almost all of the selected sections are complete within themselves, the editor has not indicated at their beginnings and endings that they are excerpts. Omissions are indicated only in the cases where two separated passages about America in a single letter are quoted with material in between omitted. While not every allusion to America in the photostatic collection has been reproduced and translated here, all references to the point of independence or immediately related considerations have been included. The original spellings of proper names have not been retained. Rayneval was spelled several ways, but Grenville was uniformly spelled Greenville. Francklin, Schelburne, Madrit, Yorck, Waschington, and Convay are typical occurrences as well as other traces of Germanic usage of the French language by some of Frederick's ambassadors, including some relatively involved sentences. The almost universal use of *Sieur* has not been translated. Sieur Lejai, for example, is rendered simply Jay. Individuals referred to in the correspondence who need identification are given explanatory footnotes at the first reference to them in all cases where the editor could identify them.   The editor has tried to keep his notes to a minimum.

The translations have been arranged chronologically.   For the benefit of the general reader three brief summaries are used to head the three chapter groupings so that the broad course of the negotiations may be seen.   The serious student is immediately referred to Samuel Flagg Bemis, *The Diplomacy of the American Revolution.*

It must be borne in mind that Prussia was a neutral during the war and that Frederick had even sought to prevent the sending of mercenaries from other German states.   After Joseph II had succeeded Maria Theresa in Austria, however, Frederick found that his former ally, Russia, was now aligned with his enemy, Austria.   Unable to break ties between Austria and France, Frederick now found himself in an isolated position and in no way able to take an unfriendly stand towards England, against whom he had grievances dating from his desertion by England in the Seven Years' War.   In fact, he even seemed to admire the work of Shelburne.   Not being a partner to the negotiations, there were a number of things he was slow to hear, and not all the information he received about American affairs was correct.   The neutral role that he was forced to play, however, accentuated the objectivity of his observations.   Aging as Frederick was and cautious as his observations had become by now, the keenness of the great Prussian was still there.

Source Note

Each of the following documents found by the editor only in the transcripts given the United States by the German government in 1881 is indicated by a dagger (†).

Each of the following documents found by the editor only in the photostatic reproductions in the Library of Congress is indicated by an asterisk (*).

Documents found by the editor in both sources are given no special designation.

American Independence through Prussian Eyes

Negotiations before the News of the Defense of Gibraltar

American negotiations for a treaty with Great Britain recognizing the independence of the thirteen states were inextricably bound up with negotiations between the British and their other enemies, the French, the Spanish, and the Dutch. While the victory of the Americans and the French at Yorktown on 19 October 1781 and the subsequent cessation of hostilities by the British against the American forces virtually assured independence, if it were to be demanded, the actual recognition was not agreed to in treaty form until 30 November 1782. Peace was eagerly awaited by Frederick, who longed for European stability and the stimulation peace could bring to Prussian commerce. In the meanwhile there remained remote chances of some kind of American settlement with Great Britain short of complete independence. Even if independence were to be granted, there remained the problems of drawing boundaries in America, the settlement of mutual debts and spoliations, the situation of the American Loyalists (a group pitied by the Prussians), the arrangement of future Anglo-American trade, the fisheries, the navigation of the American waterways, and possible British apologies relative to the conduct of the late operations.

Although the Prussians had an admirable understanding of problems involving the European balance of power, they were not always well informed about problems peculiarly American. In contemporary neutral European eyes, however, the matter of the mediation proposed by Austria and Russia loomed large. These *two empires, which as mediators, technically, signed the definitive treaties of Great Britain with France and Spain, but not the one between Great Britain and America, had consistently endeavored to be actual mediators.   Had they been able to overcome the mistrust of France and Great Britain, and had they exerted real influence on the negotiations, there is no way to be sure just how this would have affected the position of the newly independent states and their territorial claims.   Their attempts at mediation had long been going on, and their insistence was still notable in 1782 and was causing some embarrassment to the belligerents. The Prussians were also well aware that France, burdened with maintaining the expensive operations which were still going on in the Caribbean, at Gibraltar, and elsewhere, and having contributed in so large a measure to the American military success mainly for the purpose of weakening her British rival, was determined to insist on complete independence in spite of any alluring offers the British might make to their former colonists. Moreover, the American peace commissioners were rigidly bound to their ally France by their instructions of 1781.*

With the fall of Lord North's wartime ministry on 20 March 1782, separate and direct negotiations between the Americans and the British were permitted by the French on the condition that the resulting agreement be subject to the Franco-British treaty. In April these negotiations were launched in Paris by Franklin and Oswald.   Their urbane conversations were not interrupted by the fall of Rockingham's cabinet and its replacement by the more reluctant one of Shelburne in July.   Franklin then proposed the "necessary" conditions of peace, consisting of independence and evacuation, a favorable set of boundaries including the Canadian one as it was prior to the Quebec Act, and freedom for American fishermen, as well as the unlikely "desirable" articles, including indemnification for British damage, a statement by the British acknowledging their errors, the resumption of former trade advantages, and the cession of Canada.   He was joined in

August by John Jay, fresh from Madrid and suspicious of the Bourbon powers and the possibilities of arrangements they might make with the British to the disadvantage of America. The Americans, unaware of the fact that the British would grant peace on the basis of the "necessary" articles as early as the end of August, wasted time persuading the British commissioner to get his commission changed to imply independence by the new wording. By September the arrival in Paris of the Spanish minister Aranda with his proposals to divide the trans-Allegheny area between the Spanish and the British clouded the picture, and the distress of John Jay was heightened by the first mission to London of the French agent Rayneval. By the end of the month Oswald's new and still somewhat ambiguous commission had arrived, but it was followed by the news that Gibraltar in all probability could not be taken by the Bourbon powers. Frederick fully appreciated the significance of this development, which like the great victory of Rodney in the Caribbean in April had strengthened the British position, diplomatically as well as militarily.

1: *King Frederick II to Count von Lusi in London**

BERLIN, 7 January 1782

For this year your horoscope of the twenty-fifth of December may well fail to be fulfilled. Proud Albion will rather tempt her fortune once more. But if fortune is not more favorable to her than in the past, it will certainly become necessary for her to take on a more peaceful disposition. Meanwhile, America wishing to be an absolutely free republic, I strongly doubt that she will put at her head a son of His Britannic Majesty, granting to him the title of king. Besides there still remain so many articles to be arranged that it is not an easy thing to put them in order, and in the last analysis a power which has not had signal successes against its enemies can never dictate, but sees itself reduced to accepting the conditions of peace offered to it, even though **they** entail some loss.

2: *Count von Lusi to King Frederick II**

LONDON, 1 February 1782

The hope of finding an ally on the Continent seems to have vanished, and a separate peace with Holland is hardly ever mentioned any more; and furthermore the propositions made to the colonies are not of a kind to implement an agreement with the mother country, for however advantageous they may be, there is no mention made in them of independence, which remains still the Gordian Knot that cannot be untied, it appears, except by force.

3: *Lusi to Frederick II**

LONDON, 26 February 1782

The very evening of the departure of my last report [22 February 1782] the opposition proposed in the lower chamber to present a petition to the King for the discontinuation of the American war, and the motion was rejected by but one vote. General Conway, who opened this motion, resolved to renew it tomorrow, only changing the terms in order to give it a different form . . . . They claim that the ministry could avoid its fall and embarrass the opposing party by itself proposing to make peace with America, seeing that the difficulty of treating with the colonies would bring delays and give it time to take its own measures and to continue the war offensively. It may well be that the King has no liking for this expedient and would prefer to prorogue the parliament.

4: *Lusi to Frederick II**

LONDON, 1 March 1782

General Conway, seeing that the ministry's majority was so slim (as I had the honor to report in my very humble last), renewed his motion last Wednesday declaring that "the continuation of an offensive war in America with a view to reducing the colonies by force is impractical." After long debates, in a House composed of four hundred and fifty members, the opposition party carried the vote in favor of the motion by a majority of nineteen. In consequence of this superiority the House will today present a petition to the King to pray His Majesty to put an end to this war. It is impossible to predict the effect of this petition. The great question is whether to recognize the independence of America, because it is only on that condition that the colonies will accept peace. The ministry would risk, perhaps, a great deal in proposing it, and the opposition has never mentioned this independence, although yesterday certain of this party, invited by the ministry to discuss the means of making peace, said that ties of commerce and friendship could be contracted with the colonies, similar to those which Great Britain has contracted with Portugal.

The opposition will apparently oblige the King to change his ministry. It will be impossible not to dismiss them all. It is thought he will take Lord Shelburne, who has already been in the ministry, and who at the present is a protégé of the opposition. The nation is very well pleased with the parliamentary resolution, but it has not demonstrated its joy and enthusiasm as on similar occasions, although it demands and desires nothing more than peace with the colonies.

5 : *Lusi to Frederick II**

LONDON, 5 March 1782

The lower House sent (the first of the month) a numerous deputation to the King to present him with a petition by which the representatives of the nation pray him to make an end of the American war. His Majesty replied to this that he "had nothing closer to his heart than the prosperity of his people, that in consequence of the advice his Parliament had just given him he would take what measures appeared to him suitable to effect the reunion of England with her colonies in revolt, and that he would direct all his efforts against her enemies in Europe so that a peace could be obtained which would not be contrary to the prosperity and to the interests of Great Britain."

This reply having appeared too general, the House of Commons persists in the intention of ending the war in America, and General Conway introduced yesterday for this purpose a motion declaring that "whosoever dares to advocate or undertake by any means whatever continuation of the war in America, in the intention of reducing the colonies by force, shall be declared an enemy of the realm and shall be treated as such." Lord North, in opposing this motion, wished to maintain that it was superfluous and that the preceding motion (that of which I had the honor to speak to Your Majesty in my very humble last) was already quite sufficient to state the intention of the House regarding the war in America. But he could not convince any one, and the motion passed unanimously.

General Conway claimed in his address that the English troops should be left in the places which they were occupying in order to defend them in case of attack, but without acting offensively, and that as soon as possible peace negotiations with the colonies should be begun; that these negotiations would not be at all difficult to arrange since there were some Americans not far from here who were authorized to treat for peace. They say that it was Franklin at Paris and Adams at Amsterdam to whom he referred.

He said further that the colonies had not contracted any engagement with France which could prevent them from making a separate peace, but that if negotiations with them were delayed, the colonies might well accept, after all, the propositions which France has made them.

The King's idea is to continue the war in the hope of reducing the colonies by a last effort, and his ministers, interested in keeping him in this opinion, do not count as much on success as they do on gaining time, hoping that unforeseen events may bring them a way out of their difficulties. The opposition, on the contrary, seeing the successive losses, have stirred up the public's disgust with this war, and calculating the British forces to be much inferior to those of the enemy, have given the rest of the Parliament to understand that it was necessary once and for all to oppose the ministerial policy. What one should notice is that the opposition is in order, according to the constitution, and acts with boldness and persistence, which is why it does not appear that Lord North will dare present himself to the House of Commons to ask for the voting of this year's taxes, nor, in general, that the present ministry can maintain itself.

6: *Lusi to Frederick II* *

LONDON, 8 March 1782

By an act of Parliament the King has been authorized to make peace or a truce with the Americans, as he shall judge proper. This proposition, although made by a member of the ministerial party, passed by a unanimous vote. By this maneuver the ministry tried to prevent the opposition from mixing in this affair, and they claim that the King is resolved to maintain the present ministry and to make a truce with the Americans. Meanwhile the opposition bends every effort to force Lord North to quit his post and will make much trouble for him about the taxes, which he ought to propose sometime next week, and it is then that we will see whether he can manage to remain. The opposition having often said recently that there were in Europe American emissaries who were authorized to treat for peace, I tried to verify their assertions, and I found that Franklin was in correspondence on the subject with a member of the opposition, and that he had furnished the prisoner[1] in England the full powers to treat and that an agent, Lee,[2] who was in Berlin, will soon be in London. They claim that the Americans wish to come to an agreement and that they are beginning to defy the French.

7: *Frederick II to Lusi**

POTSDAM, 18 March 1782

I am astonished, I admit, to see that after the immense corruptions the King of England has made in his Parliament, the opposition has been able to gain the upper hand, as your despatch of the fifth of this month reports. But I must tell you at the same time that the project which the opposition has formed for the peace seems to me entirely impractical. A considerable body of the French are already in America, and are still being reinforced by new troops they are sending there. How, then, could they [the Americans] make peace with the English even if they wished, since the French have a superiority of all the forces in their country? Besides, the Americans wish to be independent. It is the plan in this project formed by the opposition to instal a viceroy; but demanding complete independence as they are, they will not

[1] The reference is to Henry Laurens, captured on the high seas by the British and exchanged for Cornwallis. He remained a prisoner through 1781 and arrived in Paris just in time to sign the preliminary peace with Great Britain in November of 1782.

[2] Arthur Lee was not received in either Madrid or Berlin during the war and had been recalled home.

in any wise want these conditions which England is going to offer, and all that will happen is that these propositions can cause some division among the colonies, and that is all. They would have been good to have made four years ago, but now, it appears to me, they are made too late, and the only way open to England is to make a general peace as best she can, so as not to risk losing even more of her important possessions and finding herself obliged to accumulate such prodigious debts as could not but hasten a total bankruptcy.

8: *Lusi to Frederick II**

LONDON, 19 March 1782

It is to be presumed that they [the ministry] will take measures agreeable to the public, which hopes at any price for a peace with the Americans, even under the condition of independence, provided that they can be detached from the side of France.

9: *Baron von der Goltz in Paris to Frederick II**

PARIS, 22 March 1782

Finally [there is] the news brought to Versailles by sensible people from there [America] to the effect that it would not be impossible for America, recognized as independent by England, to make arrangements in a manner which would not agree with the wishes of France. All these considerations[3] taken together

---

[3] Goltz had pointed out the embarrassing naval and military situations in which the French found themselves. In spite of the recent seizure of St. Christopher, de Grasse had rendered Martinique vulnerable by removing troops from that island for the operation. Goltz also explained that the French had not reinforced their fleet in the Caribbean although Rodney was being reinforced.

make the French ministry want to bind the Americans much tighter than they were by the treaty of alliance, which, in fact, engages this new state much less to France, than France for the benefit of it. They [the ministry] admit that in the present state of affairs it will be very much more difficult to make the Americans accept engagements than it would have been at the beginning of the troubles.

10: *Goltz to Frederick II**

PARIS, 25 March 1782

I do not know from what source the Versailles cabinet has succeeded in penetrating the true language of the Russian ministers to the Estates General about a separate peace between Holland and England, but I know that it flatters itself that it has checked this negotiation, and that the steps taken finally by Gelderland and Friesland to recognize the independence of the Americans seem well suited to embarrass the negotiators.

11: *Frederick II to Goltz**

POTSDAM, 25 March 1782

The French should undoubtedly be congratulated upon the fortunate successes of their arms in America and upon those they still have reason to expect according to your despatch of the fifteenth of this month.[4] But, in spite of that, prudence demands that the more dazzling good fortune is, the more one should be on guard lest reverses occur suddenly to bring it to nought. It is certain that the English must find themselves in very great difficulties, since having already quarreled with the American

---

[4] This despatch reported the capture of St. Christopher and the French hopes of taking Antigua.

colonies they are on the point of quarreling with the Irish also, and as for any insinuations they might make in America to bring the colonies back to them, I strongly doubt that they will succeed, since the French are the stronger there and consequently in a position to counteract them.

12: *Lusi to Frederick II**

LONDON, 26 March 1782

The opposition has just finally gained a complete victory. It refused to enter into any negotiation until it was given certainty that the former ministers would be dropped and that afterwards work would be begun on making peace with the colonies.

13: *Goltz to Frederick II**

PARIS, 29 March 1782

It is especially the nomination of Milord Shelburne[5] to the department of America [*sic*] which will give distress because people here know he enjoys the confidence of the colonies and that he has connections with more than one important person there. In the French cabinet today they feel that the Congress was not tightly enough bound by the first engagements made with it. In effect, the latter knows well how to play its game, when a new ministry will be able to offer its hand to it. This nascent power will be not only immediately independent from England, but entirely released from the court to which it owes its liberty and even free to make agreements wherever it will find them to its advantage. Although a new British ministry would

[5] Goltz reported the arrival of an emissary with a list of new cabinet members. On 25 March he indicated that the French realized the advantages a new British ministry would have for the further conduct of British affairs.

be displeasing here, they [the French] rest assured that this
change has been apparent because of the effect that it would
produce in Holland, where they hear that the desire of getting
ahead of England in the negotiation of advantageous commerce
with America warms their spirits [those of the Dutch] in favor
of independence and consequently in favor of the continuation
of the war with England.

14: *Frederick II to Lusi**

POTSDAM, 29 March 1782

It seems to me that no matter what pains they may take where
you are, they are reaching the end of their cash, and what makes
me suspect it is the discourse Villiers [Lord Clarendon] had with
you.   Here is just about the answer you can give him: that I
would be very glad to undertake the mediation between England
and her enemies, to terminate a war from which all the states of
Europe suffer indirectly, if I could see how to succeed in it.   But
there are some difficulties here which surpass my feeble gifts
and some opposing interests which I know not what expedients
could reconcile.   (1) England requires that her colonies rejoin
the mother country; France demands their independence as a
condition *sine qua non.*   (2) The colonies, even if they had the
inclination to submit to England, could not do it, in view of the
French troops, which are the strongest in America, and the
powerful reinforcements the French are sending there.   (3) The
King of Spain intends to keep Minorca and expects to take Gibraltar shortly.   How can one propose to him to relinquish his
conquests?   (4) The French have lost Pondicherry in the East
Indies [*sic*].[6]   With the successes which are accompanying their
arms, would they relinquish all expectation of compensation?

* The term *les Indes orientales* was used quite loosely in this correspondence.

(5) The Dutch, aided by Russia, are hopeful of being given back, by her mediation, certain possessions in their entirety which they lost. Can I counsel them in good faith to give up that hope, especially at a time when the victorious French are offering them guaranties and even compensations for their losses? Those are grave objections and aims so contradictory that I cannot imagine upon what would be based any propositions of accord that could be made to be acceptable to all the belligerent parties. It seems that it must be left to arms to decide these differences, and that negotiation would be insufficient to lead each of the belligerent parties to yield, each one on his own side, some part of his claims.

15: *Frederick II to Goltz**

POTSDAM, 29 March 1782

Whatever happens, meanwhile, you tell the Count de Vergennes that I have been astonished by some propositions which the English have made for me to mediate for peace between them and their enemies, to which I have replied that I saw in such a move obstacles almost insurmountable in view of the formal opposition to be found between the two belligerent parties. England wishes her colonies to be reunited, under certain conditions, to the government of Great Britain, and France demands their absolute independence. The King of Spain has taken Port Mahón[7] and still hopes to take Gibraltar. The English would like to have these possessions, and the Spanish want to keep them. France has suffered some losses in the East Indies, but as her arms have been victorious up to now on all sides, she will insist, therefore, on compensation for these losses. Holland has likewise lost in Bengal. Will England return her possessions, or will she want to keep them? All these things appear to me to be

[7] The capital of Minorca.

such that it will necessarily take a decisive turn of fortune to bring about any foundations upon which peace could be assured.

The only reflection to which this gives rise is that one could presume that England is thinking of peace, that she is feeling the horrible load with which she is burdened, and the prodigious difficulty of finding men and money; that thus she wishes to test the ground to see how she can get herself out of these difficulties and upon what conditions she can come to an agreement with France and Spain. For my part, I will be very careful not to become involved in this accord, but I think it best that they know in France in what disposition the English are to be found, and I see by your account of the eighteenth of this month that a certain ferret or emissary roves at Paris for the purpose of entering into *pourparlers.*

16: *Goltz to Frederick II**

PARIS, 1 April 1782

The power given to His Majesty in the British Parliament to negotiate with the American Confederation would cause distress here if it were exercised by a new ministry in which the Americans could be able to have confidence, but, with the present ministers, they hope at Versailles to have no fear of such a success, especially after the new advantages gained by Count de Grasse, which should more and more stiffen the Americans against the offers which the former mother country could make them. I thank Your Majesty very humbly for the information which the above mentioned *rescrit*[8] gives me about the Spanish answer to St. Petersburg, by which His Catholic Majesty continues to decline the imperial mediation, unless, according to the wishes of France, the Americans be admitted to the negotiation.

[8] Goltz referred to a *rescrit* of 19 March, which does not appear in the photostats of the Prussian Archives.

17: *Frederick II to Lusi**

POTSDAM, 1 April 1782

In regard to the English colonies in America, it could be that the English, granting them complete freedom, could be reconciled with them and retain freedom of trade in that area. . . . According to the way I envisage these affairs, the biggest mistakes of the English were, first, engaging in a civil war, which every power ought to avoid, and which can only be onerous and destructive in its consequences, and second, if she wished to make war on her colonies, she ought right away to have laid up[9] the French navy and bottled up her shipyards, which was very possible in the beginning; and meanwhile I condemn the Dutch because, being allies of England, they contracted connections with the Americans.

18: *Lusi to Frederick II**

LONDON, 2 April 1782

Up to now it is not known what measures they will take to effect a reconciliation with the colonies. Perhaps they found their hopes on the rumor which has spread here that Congress is divided against itself, and that some are discontented with the French. Besides, it is commonly believed that the Americans have made proposals for agreement to the members of Parliament who are presently at the head of affairs. The French troops in America are not strong enough to oppose the will of Congress, and France, they say, has no right to prevent the Americans from making their separate peace, being free by their treaty to come to an agreement with England, provided that independence be the basis of the agreement. The ministry and the English will agree without objection and will require nothing in return except advan-

[9] *Désarmer.*

tageous conditions for trade. A Russian courier, arriving here the twenty-ninth of last month and sent back by Simolin[10] the same day, excited a great deal of curiosity, but I have been told that he brought only the French reply, refusing to enter into negotiations, as the two imperial courts had proposed, if the English would not allow as preliminary the independence of America.

19: *Frederick II to Lusi**

POTSDAM, 4 April 1782

In regard to the continuation of the war, it will be very difficult for the mother country to come to an accord with the Americans if she does not render them independent, and should she succeed, that would not end her difficulty, for if the new ministers wish, as you point out, to continue, in spite of this, the hostilities against France and Spain, they will be obliged, in order to find the necessary funds, to create imposts very shocking and burdensome to the people.

20: *Lusi to Frederick II**

LONDON, 5 April 1782

I have heard from a good source that the ministry has sent secret emissaries to Adams at the Hague and to Franklin in Paris to open negotiations for peace. England offers to the American Confederation an alliance and a treaty of commerce, advantageous to both nations, and its troops, which are in America in case France wants to oppose a reconciliation, but they claim, what is moreover only too probable, that these emissaries have been ordered to speak neither of dependence nor independence. In any case, if this were true, this would not be the way to inspire

[10] Russian ambassador to London.

the Americans with confidence nor a trick to detach them from the side of the French, but rather an ill-advised affectation and out of season. Because it is generally known that the nation wants peace concluded on the basis of independence and that it does not hope to get it for less whatever happens, they add that the hope of success is measured by the favorable dispositions which the Americans have shown to the ministry, when it was in the opposition, and to their wish of reconciling themselves with England and to escape the tutelage of France and the imperious government of Washington, to whom they attribute ambitious views. It further remains to be known whether these ministerial suppositions are true and whether, in spite of the horrors of the war which the English have made them endure, they [the Americans] want, because of hate and mistrust of the French, to mingle with the [English] troops which until very recently were fighting them.

21: *Lusi to Frederick II**

LONDON, 9 April 1782

The negotiations with America being very secret, I have not been able to learn exactly the proposals which have been made to Congress, but it is certain that they have sent emissaries there, as I have pointed out in my previous very humble reports. General Carleton, who left some days ago to command the troops garrisoned at New York in place of Clinton, has also been instructed to negotiate in this affair on the spot and to propose there, according to what is claimed, a truce as the preliminary for a settlement.

22: *Goltz to Frederick II**

PARIS, 12 April 1782

The minister [Vergennes] spoke of the likelihood that the English ministry has already taken steps with regard to the Americans. About what I said to him that the known treaty between France and the United States[11] did not seem to bind these latter to the point where it was not to be feared that they might accept English proposals, he answered me that I was right, but that because of the testimonies, so often repeated, which Your Majesty gives of friendship for the King his master, he believed he was able to confide in me that beyond this known treaty there existed another which took from the Americans the power of treating with England about anything without the intervention of France, so that if today, as he suspected, the Court of London has offered independence to the Americans, the Congress is not able to accept it without the approbation of the Court of Versailles. Count Vergennes added that he was not ignorant of the reproaches that were made at the time that Congress was not sufficiently bound while France intervened in its behalf in such a great struggle, but that he had believed it necessary to form the ostensible treaty in order to allow England thereby the power of recognizing independence under conditions more or less troublesome for her and to open the door for a general peace, but that without doubt he would deserve the blame justly if, in effect, he had not given the Americans bonds other than those which resulted from the known treaty. I observed to Count de Vergennes that it was to be feared lest the American people, who, upon the British proposals without doubt would desire peace, would force the hand of Congress, especially if in the latter there were to be found traitors; the minister answered me that this was not impossible, but that he hoped that Congress would have suitable vigor and would

[11] The form here is *États unis;* also prevalent is *l'Amérique confédérée.* Such forms are significant.

especially understand how important it was for a new power to observe its engagements religiously and not to make its debut in the political world by grievous perfidy for its protectors. There, Sire, is the substance of this conversation in which Count de Vergennes was more open than he has been for a long while.

23: *Lusi to Frederick II**

LONDON, 16 April 1782

As for the negotiations of England with the Congress, I am assured that the Americans, mistrusting the French, have been the first to make overtures for a settlement, and that they have established as a preliminary the recognition of the King of England as their master, but that they should govern themselves by their own laws. This proposition has been very well received, as is very easy to believe, and General Carleton, who recently left for America, is charged with putting the final hand to this important affair. The confidence which the ministry testifies for the success of this negotiation makes me believe that it is not entirely without foundation.

24: *Lusi to Frederick II**

LONDON, 19 April 1782

I saw by the manner in which it expressed itself that the cabinet had not yet decided upon independence for America nor upon the manner of treating for a general peace in case separate reconciliations should not take place.

25: *Frederick II to Goltz**

POTSDAM, 22 April 1782

As for England, I doubt strongly that she will come to an agreement either with her colonies or with the Dutch. I believe, rather, that things will remain *in statu quo* both in America and in other regions, where truly the superiority of the French and the Spaniards will always give them some advantage.

26: *Goltz to Frederick II**

PARIS, 22 April 1782

The very gracious *ordre immediat* of the eighth and the *rescrit* of the ninth of this month have reached me. Your Majesty suspects that the new English ministry will be eager to offer peace to the Americans. Your Majesty will have since deigned to see in my last very humble despatches that the cabinet of Versailles foresees the same, but that Count de Vergennes believes that he has tied the hands of Congress too well for it to be able to accept a separate peace, even if England granted independence. Nevertheless, two eventualities remain ever possible; the one, that Congress break its commitments; the other, that the people force the hand of Congress. It is true that both eventualities seem hardly probable, the first because Congress could not help realizing how contemptible such a breach of faith would render the new power in the eyes of the other powers, and how much it would discourage them from any connections with it; the second because of the American people's great animosity against the English, at whose hands they have suffered so much cruelty during this war.

27 : *Lusi to Frederick II**

LONDON, 23 April 1782

We are ready, he [Fox] continued, to allow the independence
of America, and to give back to the French their establishments
in both the Indies, provided that they do the same; to cede to
Spain Minorca or Florida, or both, but we cannot cede Gibraltar,
except in the last extremity. This place, the key to the Mediterranean, would render the House of Bourbon mistress of this
sea and of the better part of the commerce of Europe.

28 : *Frederick II to Goltz**

POTSDAM, 25 April 1872

As far as I can judge, Holland will not make any separate
peace with England, because it is entirely impossible for her;
therefore France will not have much cause for concern from this
quarter, nor even from that of the English colonies in America,
who are not in any state to come to agreement with the mother
country. The Russians have indeed sent to The Hague a certain
Markov, absolutely corrupted by the English ministry. This
fellow will act with all possible vigor to bring pressure to bear
upon the Dutch, but I very much doubt that he will succeed.

29 : *Goltz to Frederick II**

PARIS, 26 April 1782

Your Majesty is surprised, and with very good reason, at
the delay in announcing the change of the English ministry
positively in my very humble despatches. Your Majesty will
not have been unaware subsequently that, because of contrary
winds, we learned of this important event several days later than

they knew it in Holland. As for the matter of immediate importance, that Your Majesty supposes the new English administration to be coming to an agreement with the Americans, the council of Versailles is equally persuaded of it, but, as I have already had the honor of stating, Count de Vergennes confided to me that according to the secret articles between France and the United States, the latter cannot accept a peace offered by England, even if England offers them independence.

30: *Goltz to Frederick II**

PARIS, 29 April 1782

The recognition which the Dutch Republic has just bestowed upon American independence should prove to England that her separate peace with Holland is a myth and thus render the English ministry more tractable for the general peace negotiations, especially when it learns that the American Congress will not regard the English offer of independence as sufficient cause for a separate peace with England. Your Majesty will have the goodness to remember that the Count de Vergennes confided to me that he had tied the hands of Congress in that particular respect. As for Your Majesty's feeling that the best interest of the belligerent powers is to agree upon peace among themselves without having recourse to the mediation of other powers, I do not believe it can be doubted that that is also the feeling of the Bourbon Courts.

31: *Lusi to Frederick II**

LONDON, 30 April 1782

France [in reply to the mediation offer of Russia and Austria] answered that as long as the King of England regards the Americans as his subjects it is not possible to enter into negotiations, but that she had nevertheless given her ministers at St. Petersburg and London orders to listen to what England and the mediating courts wish to propose. Upon this answer the ministers of the two imperial courts have been ordered by their courts to ask the Court of London for the same full powers for her ministers to open negotiations. Fox has not failed to inform me of the request [to mediate] on the part of the above mentioned courts. He added that he would not reply until the end of the week; that the British ministry did not count on peace very much from this negotiation, but that it felt itself, in order not to irritate the mediating powers, obliged to give a satisfactory answer, and that, for this effect, it will admit the independence of the united provinces [*sic*] including New York, South Carolina, and Georgia, that it will propose reciprocal restitution of captured provinces, and that on these principles it will give full powers to Keith [in Vienna]. Meanwhile, Fox tells me, the mediators will apply themselves to settle these affairs. We [English] will try through Grenville, a young man of much worth, who is now in Paris, to obtain in as far as possible, secret negotiations. But in case this project miscarries, he continued, to the point where the King your master should want to enter into the negotiations— I answered him that knowing the sincere desire of Your Majesty to re-establish the peace, I could give assurance that you would not refuse to contribute to it. I told him what you had instructed me in your direct orders. He was very flattered to see that the advice of Your Majesty for obtaining peace conformed to the measures which they had taken for this purpose and told me that if it were necessary to open a congress, all possible would be done to prevent it from assembling at Vienna, and the British ministry will continue to have the same confidence in the knowledge and friendship of Your Majesty, and he will still wait some time to see the course affairs will take in order to give me the above mentioned statement, of which I made mention in my last despatch, and in the meanwhile he will communicate all that takes place in these negotiations.

32: *Frederick II to Lusi**

POTSDAM, 2 May 1782

In the gazettes there is a declaration which the King has made to the lower House according to which he blames all past mistakes on his preceding ministry and declares that he intends to govern by the advice and consent of the present. I am astonished all the more at this declaration, because the King of England is stiff and obstinate in his feelings. If you can [uncover] some information about the effect that is made on him by the change and the new policy which he embraces, I would be very glad to be informed of it.

33: *Goltz to Frederick II**

PARIS, 6 May 1782

Your Majesty having predicted perfectly the slight success of England's peace overtures to the Dutch, I can only refer to what I subsequently had the honor to report concerning the satisfaction of France at the Dutch refusal of this proposition of separate peace. In six weeks or two months it will probably be known that the Court of London has been no more fortunate in dealing with the Americans, even while offering them independence.

34: *Goltz to Frederick II* *

PARIS, 10 May 1782

I have received your very gracious direct order of the twenty-fifth and the *rescrit* of the twenty-seventh. As Your Majesty has the grace to say in the former, Markov has been known here ever since his nomination to The Hague as a zealous partisan of the British cause, as I reported at the time. Since then the secret conferences which he arranged with an English emissary, Wentworth, have not passed unnoticed. Now that the Republic has recognized American independence and that its response to the English peace proposals has been to decline them, they fully expect here to keep Holland among the number of the enemies of England until the general peace. But since the aforesaid recognition of independence will no longer be a difficulty as soon as England herself has offered it to America, the latest advice given to the Duke de la Vauguyon[12] is to the effect that if it is perceived that even the consideration of seeing many of their possessions in the hands of the French does not have sufficient effect upon the Dutch, he, as ambassador, is authorized to offer a formal alliance; however this would only be a last resort. . . . Concerning what has been seen in some newspapers, that the district of Vermont, between New York and Canada, had been made an offer by General Haldimand,[13] the English governor, to return under British domination, Doctor Franklin gives assurance that this report is entirely false, and that according to his letters of 22 March, of a more recent date consequently, the Congress had no suspicion of such a defection.

[12] French ambassador to The Hague.
[13] He was in command at Quebec and had for some time been involved in separate British negotiations with Vermont that had begun as early as 1779.

35: *Answer to the Court of Spain**
(To the offer of mediation by Russia and Austria)

(Filed after a despatch from Lusi, dated London, 10 May 1782)
(Received from Count Belgioioso, 28 April 1782)

PARDO, 14 January 1782

The King, intimately persuaded of the rectitude and the sincerity of the intentions of the two Imperial Courts of Vienna and Russia, reiterates protestations of his recognition of the offices which the two courts repeat in regard to the belligerent powers. These offices obviously prove their ardent wishes for peace, since in spite of the difficulties presented by the answer of the English ministry, in which it refuses in substance the proposition of the High Mediators with a very noticeable kind of dryness or harshness, they conceal it with a grandeur of spirit in order to attain the goal which they propose for the advantage of Europe and even for all mankind.

The King, wishing therefore to contribute as much as he can to a goal so laudable and so desired, has pondered with much reflection the above-mentioned answer of the Court of London; and seeing that they do not contest in it the explanations concerning the interests of Spain, which this power has requested in order to acquiesce in the proposal of the High Mediators, and that the British ministry has reduced the subject of its answer to refusing any treaty with the American colonies in a congress under any mediation whatever, the King has nothing to add and no modification to make in his explanations as long as England will neither combat nor modify these nor accept clearly and positively. And this being the case, the ambassador of the King at Vienna has henceforth the order to listen to the overtures which are made to him and the expedients which are proposed to him, and to establish negotiations as soon as he is assured of bases sufficient and capable of leading to a happy issue conforming to the principles set forth before and to the explanations given.

Among these explanations the King repeats the following, to wit: that His Majesty will not be able to accede to any treaty nor approve of any congress unless France be in agreement and satisfied with the manner of treating the article about the colonies.

36: *Answer of the Court of France** *(To the offer of mediation by Russia and Austria)*

(Filed after a despatch from Lusi, dated London, 10 May 1782) (Received from Count Belgioioso, 28 April 1782)

[VERSAILLES?], 5 February 1782

The King has received with as much sensibility as gratitude the response of the two mediating courts. His Majesty regards it as a new proof of their good will for him, of the justice which they give to his faith in their impartiality, and of the true interest which they take in the prompt re-establishment of peace.

The King has not wavered nor will he waver in the desire of favoring such salutary views, and the two High Mediators may be assured that it will never depend on His Majesty, where he is concerned, that they not be immediately in a position to give free rein to their benevolent zeal.

But the Court of London removes every means and all hope of the King in this regard by its unalterable resolution to regard the Americans as its subjects; such resolution renders useless every attempt that could be made for peace. It destroys the plan of the two mediators from top to bottom, since it prejudices in the most pre-emptory manner the question which provides the subject of the quarrel and of which the decision, directly or indirectly, should be the basic preliminary for the future peace.... His Majesty believes it necessary to observe that he has allies with whom he has inviolable commitments, and that he would betray them in abandoning the American cause, and that he would abandon this cause if he should bring himself to negotiate a separate peace independently of the United States. The High Mediators have felt the impossibility of this line of action, since they have themselves proposed to set in motion on an equal footing the negotiations of the King and those of the United States. But, even supposing that the King should stand aside from the American affairs, that he content himself with arranging his own personal interests, and that he leave to the Americans the task of reaching an agreement with the former mother country, what will be the result of such conduct? The result will be, obviously, that the peace will be illusory, that it will be an *être de raison (sic)*. In fact if, as appears from the greatest evidence, the Americans persist in their refusal to return under the rule of the British Crown, the war will continue between England and her former colonies, and the King will be obliged then, as he is at the present, to assist them.

37: *Sandoz-Rollin*[14] *to Frederick II**

PARIS, 13 May 1782

SIRE!

You may consider as certain and secret, my English correspondent has just written me, that Grenville left for Paris on April twenty-fifth. His object is to sound the Bourbon Courts about a general peace and to propose some articles, the gist of which follows, as I promised you: (1) A truce with America for eighteen months at the end of which, if the Americans persist in their separation from the mother country, independence will be recognized and pronounced. (2) English and French troops will be withdrawn from the American continent as soon as the preliminaries are signed; the French resident minister to the Congress

[14] The Prussian legation secretary in Paris.

will be recalled, until the expiration of the above mentioned truce, and will be sent back at that time if independence is confirmed. (3) Reparations to be made to France and Spain will not be discussed and determined until these preliminary articles are agreed upon and accepted as the base of the negotiations, England having cause to expect justice and generosity from His Most Christian Majesty, and that he will not demand anything that could wound the dignity of the English Crown, but on the contrary will seek to persuade his ally, Spain, to the same way of feeling. (4) The Dutch Republic will be included in the general peace, and France will not put any obstacle in the way of the confirmation and reinstatement of earlier treaties which are in force between England and the Republic. Acting upon this information, I was at once on the lookout to discover whether Grenville had arrived at Paris. He had indeed, and two days later he had a secret conference with the Marquis [*sic*] de Vergennes to which the Spanish minister was called. The conference lasted nearly three hours. Without knowing what went on there and what the result was, I learned only that they are busy in the *bureaux* formulating other preliminary terms to serve as a reply to those from the Court of London and that Grenville would probably be charged with delivering them to his court.

I am, Sire,

With the deepest respect, Your Majesty's
Very humble, very obedient, and very faithful servant and
   subject,[15]

SANDOZ-ROLLIN

38: *Lusi to Frederick II**

LONDON, 17 May 1782

Fox told me confidentially that Count de Vergennes had answered Grenville that the independence of America was not

[15] This was the form used consistently in all despatches.

a concession made to France and gave him to understand that the basis upon which the English want to treat would not suffice; but since he did not reveal himself further in this first interview, it will be necessary to see in the sequel what are the views of the French ministry, and the intentions of Spain, whose reply had not yet arrived at Versailles . . . . Meanwhile, Franklin had written to Fox that the object of the war no longer existed, and that he no longer saw any obstacle to the return of peace, which makes the ministry hope that if the French required too much it would be possible to detach the Americans from the alliance. All that will be made clear in a short time.

39: *Lusi to Frederick II**

LONDON, 24 May 1782

As for the negotiations of Grenville, things are about where they were. Count de Vergennes continues to reject negotiations based on the principles the English propose. The English do the best they can to detach the Americans from the French alliance. Oswald, who has been sent as a courier to Paris for this purpose and who acts in concert with Grenville, has returned expressly in order to tell the ministry that Franklin had expressed the hope to him that in case France should not want peace and America be declared independent by England, the thirteen provinces would make their separate peace, not believing themselves obliged to act in concert with France to sustain the pretensions of Spain and Holland. The ministry sent Oswald back to assure Franklin that they would grant to the Americans all that they ask, and that they had already given orders to evacuate New York and Charleston. Whatever the British ministry thinks about it, it is scarcely probable that the special settlement with America will take place and that France will not sign a general peace. She must be just as exhausted from the war as England.

40 : *Sandoz-Rollin to Frederick II**

PARIS, 27 May 1782

The courier from Grenville had been gone only three days when I at once received a letter from my English correspondent to the following effect: France demands the pure and simple independence of America without any modification, His Majesty not wishing to allow that his minister be temporarily recalled, or that there be any truce between America and England.

41 : *Goltz to Frederick II**

PARIS, 28 May 1782

I can add nothing today to my last two very humble despatches, so I will go on to the negotiations of Grenville, the English emissary. I am assured that these overtures deal principally with the following points: a truce of eighteen months and a cessation of hostilities, during which time France would withdraw her minister to the American Congress, and England meanwhile considering what she can do about recognizing American independence; withdrawal respectively of their troops from that continent; the cession of Gibraltar to Spain in exchange for Ceuta.[16] This last point must not have been advanced by Grenville as anything but an idea of his own in line with what he had said he had perceived of the ideas of the British ministry. I have been assured that the reply of the Court of Versailles was: that they would not stickle at the truce, but that they held the recognition of American independence pure and simple to be indispensable; that consequently the English demand to have the French minister to the Congress recalled was inadmissible; that regarding the exchange of Gibraltar for Ceuta, it could neither be foreseen whether His Catholic Majesty would relish the proposal, nor whether the

[16] A port on the Moroccan coast opposite from Gibraltar.

position of this latter place would not be less favorable for England than that of Gibraltar. That, according to what I have been told, was the reply with which Grenville despatched an express to London. One for him arrived three days ago, but it is still not known whether it was in reply to what he sent, or whether it contained simply the news of Admiral Rodney's great success of April 12.[17]

42: *Lusi to Frederick II**

LONDON, 4 June 1782

If her [France's] demands are tolerable in the least, we [Fox is being paraphrased] will consent to them, but if she wants to take advantage of our good intentions in order to raise her claims, and if Holland continues to follow the lead of the cabinet of Versailles, in this case we will beg the aid of the King, your master, and that of Russia, and we are sure that being aided by these two powers we will also have the support of Denmark. He told me of this last country as if they had already sounded her and she had given hopes of entering into the views of the English ministry, provided that they were supported by some other ally. I answered him that England could hardly flatter herself that she would be aided by Russia, seeing that the Emperor [of Austria] is seeking to form a triple alliance between himself, France, and Russia. He answered me that he did not doubt that the Emperor was on the side of France but that he would be surprised to see Russia abandon England, that she [Russia] had, moreover, made the strongest representations by her ministers at The Hague in order to cause the Republic to make a separate peace with us, and that she expressed herself in the most friendly terms here through her minister and at St. Petersburg vis-à-vis [the British ambassador] Harris. Moreover, Sire, I have observed that these people

[17] On this date Rodney defeated de Grasse in the Caribbean.

will continue the war willingly if they can make a separate peace with Holland, and that they imagine that Your Majesty could aid in this, because, with regard to the Americans, the ministry seems to be sure of being able to detach them from the side of France.

43 : *Lusi to Frederick II**

LONDON, 14 June 1782

Lord Clinton arrived day before yesterday from New York. I do not know yet if he brought any interesting news, but it is widely stated that Carleton had arrived four or five days before the departure of Clinton, and that the Congress and the Americans had expressed much joy over hearing of the ministerial change and the resolution of Parliament not to make war any further in America.

44: *Goltz to Frederick II**

PARIS, 14 June 1782

Grenville received full powers at the same time, but this formality will not help him if he cannot present a more satisfactory basis for negotiation. Up to this time France seems very determined to reject any other basis than full recognition of American independence, not merely as a sequel of the negotiations during a truce, nor even as an object of negotiation to be discussed between the House of Bourbon and Great Britain, but as a preliminary without which she will not listen to overtures on any other subjects. As this form of recognition is undoubtedly somewhat repugnant to the Court of London, since it makes that court appear to be forced to it, this point alone seems sufficient to put off the peace.

45 : *Frederick II to Goltz*

POTSDAM, 24 June 1782

But to come to affairs in general, I must conjecture from everything that has reached me that the war will still continue this year and even next year; that France would not want the mediation of Russia, nor England that of the Emperor, and that consequently the belligerent parties will make peace without the intervention of anyone, but not before resources are exhausted on both sides. This is all that I am able to tell you today in reply.

46 : *Goltz to Frederick II*

PARIS, 24 June 1782

As for the negotiating of Grenville, the statements which this emissary conceals here from everyone certainly conform to those which, according to the *rescrit* I am acknowledging, the British ministry is making on the probability of a general peace coming very soon. But I believe that basically these negotiations are no further advanced than my last very humble reports showed them.

47 : *Frederick II to Goltz*

POTSDAM, 27 June 1782

As far as large questions are concerned I can see that the English and French will not be able to agree, as it usually happens, one side demanding too much, and the other side wanting to give too little.

Here is another question I am going to put to you, to which, however, I am assured in advance you will give me as little answer as to the previous ones. It is whether the financial condition of France will permit her to make as costly a campaign in the coming year as she is carrying on at the present.

48 : *Lusi to Frederick II**

LONDON, 28 June 1782

The British ministry has received the answer of the Versailles cabinet to Grenville's proposals. France accepts the three points England proposes as the basis of the negotiation, to wit: the independence of America, the mutual restitution of conquests, and the Treaty of Paris [1763] as the base on which settlements will be made to end the differences which could block a peace. . . . Meanwhile they suspect that this answer is no other than a subterfuge for delaying the negotiations until the end of the campaign. It is hardly likely that the English will wait until this time. Rather they will insist on an explicit answer for continuing to negotiate seriously or to break the *pourparlers* entirely. In the latter case the ministry flatters itself with the possibility of inducing the Americans to make a separate peace, which would be more agreeable to the nation than a general peace. As for the mediation, there is no news of the steps of the two mediating courts, but it is rather thought that the Emperor [of Austria] does not show any more the same eagerness to be mediator of the general peace.

49 : *Goltz to Frederick II*

PARIS, 28 June 1782

Grenville received another express today. I have been assured that he got full powers to negotiate conjointly with the French ministry, the minister of Spain, and Franklin. That doubtless will lessen the proper mistrust which overtures made separately to the three powers would give, but still nothing is changed in regard to the basic proposals. It is apparent that here they [the French] will require independence pure and simple for America. But with however much pains they may seem to want not to deviate from this point, they want just as much not to break off the negotiations of this British emissary, and I think as much as ever that they will agree to suspend them for the present and take them up again toward the end of the campaign. It is claimed, in fact, that Secretary of State Fox is of the opinion that if at the end of the specified term, the beginning of August, the enemies of England have not accepted the overtures of His Britannic Majesty, the English will no longer feel themselves bound and will return their interests into the hands of the mediating courts. This insinuation could have some effect at Versailles, for, although they well know there that at heart England must prefer a direct negotiation to that of mediators, at the same time they fear the intervention of the latter even more at Versailles than at London. I know that the minister of Russia is very disturbed about the negotiation of Grenville. He was not able to conceal it even from me, and let drop to me a remark on what a contradiction the haste of England to send an envoy here afforded to that country's actions toward the two Imperial Courts.

50: *Lusi to Frederick II**

LONDON, 5 July 1782

The principles of the administration of Lord Shelburne differ from those of the Marquis of Rockingham only with regard to the management of the realm's internal problems; it is indeed maintained that he has always been against the independence of America, but there is, however, no proof of the sentiments that are attributed to him in this regard. And supposing that he had them, I do not believe that the British ministry would be able to withdraw the proposals made with so much solemnity to the American colonies. This revolution not being finished, time will tell us how they are going to choose to manage things, and I hope to make a more detailed report about this to Your Majesty by my next regular despatch, but it is probable that they will not discard the system which has been followed up to the present, and that the ministry will continue to make every effort to form this triple alliance.[18]

51: *Goltz to Frederick II*

PARIS, 5 July 1782

The ambassador of the Emperor and the Russian minister have just renewed at Versailles the offer of the mediation of their courts for the general peace. Count de Vergennes has answered that in order to give a formal reply, he will ask for the King's orders as soon as possible; but that meanwhile he was able to give assurances that France continued to have the greatest confidence in the two Imperial Courts and their good intentions of contributing to the re-establishment of peace; but that he should, however, recall to them the desire of England to negotiate directly with her enemies. Perhaps this minister will stick to this answer; but in the case that he should give one more revealing, I count on learning of it by the same means which gave me this one. Moreover, I know that when the Russian minister wished to learn the British proposals, Count de Vergennes buttoned himself up completely. I have been assured that although the French cabinet does not communicate all the details of the negotiations with Grenville to Vienna, it believes, however, it should tell Vienna the gist of them, but Prince Kaunitz is not altogether satisfied

[18] Great Britain had been seeking support from Russia, Prussia, and also Denmark. For the British awareness of Frederick's caution about such an alignment in 1782, see Friedrich Kapp, *Friedrich der Grosse und die Vereinigten Staaten* (Leipzig, 1871), pp. 81-82.

with this.   Nevertheless it seems all the more here that this half-way confiding on the part of the Court of Vienna will have to suffice, since it is believed certain that the cabinet of London has not given out a word [to them] about the mission of Grenville. It is believed that when lately the envoy of England poured out strong complaints to Prince Kaunitz about the refusal of Holland to reach a settlement with his court, this statesman indicated to him his surprise about his complaints at a moment when England is alienating herself from the mediating courts, as I have had the honor to report previously.   Your Majesty will deign to see that the cabinet of Versailles wants to appear to desire the intervention of the mediators, although actually it would be even more angry than England to be obliged to place reliance in them.   As for the negotiations of Grenville, I have reason to believe them still at the point of which I have recently spoken; that is to say that unless a great event takes place, be it in the East Indies or in the Antilles, these negotiations will probably drag out until the end of this campaign.   In America there could scarce-ly be any great developments, because of the reasons I have already explained before in detail.   A Jamaica expedition no longer seems possible this year, but also a decided superiority of seven or eight ships of the line and a very great superiority in ground forces, on the side of the allies, should not cause one to fear that the English will want to take the offensive.   Such seems to me to be the opinion of the best informed people . . . . [An American, Jay, employed in Spain until now, has just arrived here. It is believed that he has been sent to assist Franklin in case the peace negotiations take complete shape.   Your Majesty knows of the suspicion there is that England will propose to the Ameri-cans to grant them the same status as is at present enjoyed by Ireland.   They are worried at Versailles as to whether the Congress really will want to hold to the treaty with France and refuse in consequence all offers which do not recognize uncondi-tional independence; they fear, I say, that the above-mentioned

English proposition could cause great ferment in the minds of the Americans.][19]

52: *Goltz to Frederick II*

PARIS, 8 July 1782

My very humble reports, especially that of the fifth of this month, only reaffirm Your Majesty's view that peace this year is unlikely. As for the new offer of mediation of the two Imperial Courts, their desire to intervene is animated naturally because of the fear of not being appealed to in this matter. Your Majesty will have the goodness to see the pains the French ministry takes to persuade them, since the arrival of Grenville, that it is not France but England which prefers direct negotiations. What seconds them well in this regard is that this English emissary had already been sent by his court, when, on the twenty-eighth of April, his court caused to be declared at St. Petersburg that they still desired to see the mediators intervene. At Versailles they hope that the seeming inconsistency of these two steps taken at the same time will cool the favorable interest of the Tsarina of Russia for the Court of London, especially if the latter had formerly promised considerable advantages to Russia in recompense for the mediation in which it has now frustrated her [Catherine II]. Under the ministry of Count Panin[20] this result would have been yet much more assured; but they make no secret today of the care that Prince Potemkin,[21] and all his party, so devoted to the Courts of Vienna and London, will take to lessen the dissatisfaction of the Tsarina of Russia in this regard. I have nothing to add here to what I had the

[19] The passage between the brackets is added from the *Facsimiles from German Archives, Preussisches Geheimes Staatsarchiv, Berlin-Dahlem,* Library of Congress, Washington, D. C.

[20] Count Nikita Panin was formerly minister of foreign affairs.

[21] Prince Potemkin was minister of war.

honor of reporting lately about the languor which will probably characterize the negotiating of Grenville until news of America and especially the East Indies arrives. If what was announced in clear [not coded] is confirmed, there is no doubt that they will be obstinate at Versailles in asking that all be restored in India as it was in 1755, a request which will not seem to the English easy to grant, because it would end this source of immense wealth for them. Some days ago here the curtain was raised on a new theater on the coasts, and it is apparent that in spite of the superiority of the combined fleet [French and Spanish] they will seek out the enemy even in the English Channel, where he has the great advantage of his own ports, but considering the lively valor of Lord Howe, it would not be surprising if he came out of the Channel to fight.

53: *Frederick II to Goltz*

POTSDAM, 8 July 1782

I have received your report of 28 June. I see the impossibility of making peace which faces France as long as the seige of Gibraltar continues; but I believe additionally that the French and the English are still rather far apart in their claims, as much in regard to the total independence of the colonies as to the indemnifications that France will want to have for her losses, and that the King of Spain, even if he does not capture Gibraltar, may demand that it be given him at the peace. Thus, whatever happens, this campaign will probably run its course, and it will not be until it has that one will be able to see whether dispositions will be animated by pacific thoughts or whether martial fury will carry them still further. But I am beginning to believe that France, her allies, and England will be wise enough to avoid all foreign mediation and to reach a settlement among themselves conforming to their interests. At this moment, however, it is still impossible for things to reach a conclusion.

54: *Goltz to Frederick II*

PARIS, 12 July 1782

As for the negotiation of Grenville, I dare to refer to my last very humble despatches which announce it much less advanced than the British ministry wants it believed to be. Your Majesty has the goodness to tell me that England must have positively promised the Bourbon powers the independence of America and besides asked on what conditions they desire the peace. On the first point Your Majesty will have already deigned to see that not only do they not believe at Versailles in the good faith of England about the recognition of independence, but they also suppose that England is negotiating in America to keep that country by allowing it the privileges Ireland has. It is true that Grenville insinuated that Parliament would soon grant the formal proclamation of independence, but since at Versailles, they suspected those insinuations to be a lure to bring about direct negotiations between France and England, they wanted first to wait and see whether in fact this important formality and this parliamentary act, since Parliament is about to adjourn, would not be put off until it reconvenes. To that which I had the honor to report lastly, about the new steps of the Imperial Courts in offering their mediation, I can add the following facts: they know more than ever at Versailles that although Russia took a real and lively interest in the separate peace between England and Holland, she is entirely passive about the general peace; that the Tsarina of Russia relies in that matter on the advice of the Court of Vienna to the point that when Prince Kaunitz[22] warns

[22] Austrian foreign minister.

Prince Gallitzin[23] of a step he desires to take in regard to France relative to this mediation, this latter prince according to an order of the Tsarina, given once for all, instructs Prince Bariatinsky to join with the ambassador of Vienna here in the action. I need not add that this secondary role, which the Tsarina is content to play, seems to the Versailles ministry to correspond but poorly to the dignity which this princess is so pleased to affect in other respects. If, at all times, [the ministry] at Versailles has desired to decline the mediation and to prefer to it a direct negotiation with the enemy, it now has a new reason for discontent with the Court of Vienna. Baron de Breteuil[24] knew for several weeks that according to despatches from London to Prince Kaunitz, the latter could take up again the responsibility of offers of mediation. The French ambassador was surprised by the silence of the Austrian minister, who did not break his silence until the instant after the news of the defeat of Count de Grasse, and then when he did so, added some reflections on the probability that this event rendered the Bourbon Courts less difficult about making peace. Baron de Breteuil felt that he could not dispense with replying to Prince Kaunitz that although he did not yet know the feelings of the King his master relative to this event, he thought that he could guarantee that this monarch knew too well the extent of his means for this day to have any further effect than to cause him to redouble his efforts. As for the above-mentioned despatches, communicated so tardily by Prince Kaunitz, the substance of them was not a request for a congress, but merely the consent of England in case the mediators should succeed in disposing the enemies of His Britannic Majesty to a congress. The reply of Spain is now awaited here so that that of France may be given conjointly with it. According to all appearances, they will

[23] Prince Dmitri Mihailovich Gallitzin, ambassador to Vienna, not to be confused with Prince Dmitri Alexevich Gallitzin, who, together with Markov, who joined him in March 1782, represented Russian interests at the Hague.

[24] French ambassador to Vienna.

be like those given many times before on the same subject, which were that the assembling of a congress seemed useless as long as England, because of conditions plainly enunciated, would not provide a basis for negotiation. If, in order to avoid mediation, the Bourbon Courts continually replied thus to the Imperial Courts before England opened a direct negotiation here, they will with more reason continue this line today. We must see whether this is the last time the Imperial Courts will offer their mediation, without believing any longer that any of the belligerent powers sincerely desires it.

55: *Lusi to Frederick II* *

LONDON, 12 July 1782

Fox has not explained in what way the ministry set aside the principles that were followed at the start, but it is known that he does not share the sentiments of Lord Shelburne, the latter wishing to negotiate with America on the same basis as had been the case with Ireland, or at least not to grant absolute independence to the Americans, except as the price of peace. While, instead, Fox holds the opinion that independence ought to be granted to America without making a treaty with her, imagining that this generous course would cause the colonies in gratitude to bind themselves forever to England. Whatever these differences may be, the Duke of Richmond and General Conway, who are both of the same party as Fox, have had naturally to justify in Parliament why they have not resigned their places. The latter especially did this with considerable skill. He declared that he kept his post because he did not see that the ministry was discarding the principles that had been established when he assumed his duties. These principles were: (1) To grant unconditionally absolute independence to America. (2) To establish a system of economy in all departments of the government.

(3) To remove from the Crown the means of increasing its influence in Parliament through corruption. Finally, to assure to Ireland, in the most straightforward manner, the constitution and independence which have been granted her.

The Duke of Richmond likewise declared that the absolute independence of America would not be an obstacle to the peace; but Lord Shelburne has not explained himself as clearly on that point. He has been content to say that the independence of the colonies was a great misfortune for England and for America, and one which can be justified only by necessity. However, it is not to be presumed that it is necessary to interpret these vague expressions as a resolution to continue the war with the purpose of reducing the colonies to obedience. The proposals made to France, which they can scarcely withdraw, at least prove the contrary; and Lord Shelburne has himself told me that they will not be changed, so that it will depend on France and her allies to put an end to this war in accepting just conditions. Lord Shelburne is known, moreover, as a man of great skill who is able to adjust himself to circumstances, and who makes a good thing of having been a friend of Chatham[25] and his policy; but it would be sad for humanity and for England in particular if he wanted to continue the war until he had brought the nation back to the glorious situation in which Chatham had placed her during his administration.

The secretary of state for foreign affairs has not yet been named, but it is believed at the present that it will be Lord Grantham, of whom much good is said, and who has been ambassador in Spain. As for other posts, there has been one change: Thomas Townshend has replaced Lord Shelburne as secretary of state for internal affairs. He has been heretofore secretary of war and seems to be a man of skill. He has inclined at times towards the party of sure patriots, which was Rockingham's, and at other times to the party of those who would give to the Crown a limited

[25] Pitt the Elder, prime minister during the Seven Years' War.

influence, like that of Shelburne. The young Pitt, of whom I made mention in my last despatch, has been made Chancellor of the Exchequer, which may be considered as the principal minister of the prime minister.[26]

Yesterday the King prorogued the two houses, which probably will not reassemble until November. During this time the ministry will be able to undertake whatever it wishes without having to fear any opposition. But next winter the opposition will perhaps be formidable, and it will be greatly to the credit of Lord Shelburne if he is able to resist it, which will depend on the measures that he takes to make peace and on the success of the military operations during this campaign.

In the meantime, the hope of making a special agreement with America has also vanished. Letters which arrived yesterday from New York report that the Congress refuses to treat with General Carleton, not wanting to make peace without the participation of its allies. The general assemblies of Maryland, New York, Pennsylvania, and Virginia have resolved that any proposal made by the enemy to the United States, or to any one of the provinces in particular, for a peace or a truce separate from its allies, will be regarded as insidious and inadmissible. It is therefore a general peace that will put an end to this war; but on what can the hope of seeing it established be based if France insists on her demands and Spain on the cession of Gibraltar?

56: *Goltz to Frederick II*

PARIS, 15 July 1782

The information, however indirect, of the advantages gained in February by French arms in India seems to become more and more probable. That engagement alone, as I told you on the

[26] The words were *Chef de la Trésorerie*. The First Lord of the Treasury is the prime minister.

eighth, would be in fact already quite important in itself, but it is hoped that it will bring to Versailles the most marked consequences against the enemy, since de Bussi will have been able to begin land operations and again stir up the efforts of Hyder Ali,[27] while the squadron attacks the establishments of the coast and islands. They seem at last to realize more and more at Versailles a truth of which perhaps they ought to have been aware for a long time much more than they have been, which is that it is in this part of the world that the blows most felt by England can be dealt. I am quite ready to believe that the desire to wrest from the latter this source of wealth, which has indeed contributed so much to its greatness during the last thirty years, occupies the French ministry fully as much, at least at the present moment, as the fate of its allies, the Americans, although the latter point is emphasized much more in the negotiations with Grenville than the article concerning India. The truth of my suspicion in this respect will soon be determined, since Fox has just answered to the House of Commons that the opinion of the entire British ministry is in favor of the independence of America; this announcement seems intended to precede by only a short interval the formal bill of recognition. Your Majesty will deign to remember that Versailles has consistently refused to enter into the negotiations proper until this bill has appeared; thus if it is now going to appear, and afterwards Versailles still continues to turn a deaf ear to the overtures of Grenville, then the East Indies [*sic*] must be the real object of France.

As for the Antilles, I think that no new development is expected at present. The engagement of 12 April[28] has doubtless caused the cancellation of the expedition to Jamaica, but also it is not to be feared that the victor of that day can undertake anything against any of the possessions of the allies. The forces

[27] For years Hyder Ali held power in Mysore under the Maharajah. After some success in 1782 he met defeat and death.

[28] The original has 19 April but undoubtedly refers to the victory of Rodney on 12 April.

of the latter, assembled at Santo Domingo, will compensate in their movements for those of their enemy at Jamaica. The Marquis de Bouillé[29] is holding frequent conversations with the ministry and the ambassador from Spain, and sometimes with the King himself. I expect more than ever the return of this general to the islands soon, and that if the peace treaty is not made, he will be put in command of the expedition to Jamaica this winter.

57: *Frederick II to Lusi**

POTSDAM, 18 July 1782

I understand that for the most part those who have just taken office will scarcely be able to avoid the course of their predecessors, but if they do not want to consent to the independence of the Americans, which is an affair already far advanced, they will fall into a labyrinth from which they will scarcely be able to find the way out.

58: *Goltz to Frederick II**

PARIS, 19 July 1782

It is known that the emissary sent to the American Congress by General Carleton, at the time of his landing in New York, has not even been received by them; Doctor Franklin told me yesterday that Congress had replied to the English government that as the interests of the United States were intimately connected with those of her allies, the ministers resident with them in Europe had the full powers to negotiate, and that therefore the Congress would not be able to enter into any discussion. Jay, who for several years has been employed by the Congress in Spain, left

[29] He was the governor of Martinique.

a chargé d'affaires there and came here to assist Doctor Franklin; it was thought at first after the change in the British ministry in March that the garrisons on the American continent would be transferred in large part to the Antilles. This reduces now to about two thousand men the New York garrison; a larger number were embarked afterwards but were landed again.

59: *Lusi to Frederick II**

LONDON, 19 July 1782

[Fox stated in a speech] that the nation believed in good faith that Lord Shelburne would consent to the independence of America, because he declared that he believed this concession necessary. But [Fox said] this declaration should not be believed by anyone, because that gentleman has all along been opposed in the most solemn manner to the independence of the colonies, and he has said very expressly in the Upper House that he will never give his consent to it and that he will regard as a traitor to the country anyone who dares to propose it, no matter how sad may be the state to which England may be reduced.

Fox concluded from this that one is in no way able to put one's confidence in the words of him who professes opinions so contrary. He gives assurance, besides, that he has very clearly observed that the ministry has discarded the principles which had been established as the base of the system that should be followed in the cabinet, and that indeed it was that situation which had determined him to resign, in order to give warning to the nation and call attention to the danger which menaces it. However, the speaker confesses that he does not know the plan that Count [*sic*] Shelburne proposes to follow at the present in regard to the colonies, but that he has said recently that he regarded the independence of America as an eclipse which would obscure the glory of Great Britain, and that at the very least it would be necessary to grant it conditionally and make it the basis of any treaty. Fox opposes this opinion, and he does not believe that the absolute independence of America would be the end of the glory of his country, and he maintains that the manner in which this independence is granted will be more important for the future than independence itself. . . .

Whatever Fox says about it, I believe that the ministry is thinking seriously of peace, and in order not to oppose the wishes of the nation, it will grant America absolute independence.

60 : *Goltz to Frederick II*

PARIS, 22 July 1782

The very gracious direct order of the eighth and the *rescrit* of the ninth of this month have come to me.

Your Majesty deigns to inform me that in fact, as I had the honor of announcing, the negotiations of Grenville were never so far advanced as was said in the letters from London, which were in accordance with what the British ministry took care to let on in this regard. The difference in principles between Lord Shelburne and Fox with regard to America, so well known today since the withdrawal of the latter, was alone enough to interrupt the aforesaid negotiations, but Your Majesty will have the goodness to recall that apart from this point I have suspected that something still more important for France was yet an obstacle for the peace at the present moment; I speak of the East Indies.[30] At present, since Grenville has been recalled to London, we must wait to see whether the negotiations are broken completely or whether this negotiator will return with new instructions. I am led to believe the former, unless Lord Shelburne suddenly allows the recognition of the independence of America without restriction, and even if he should come to this, the formal parliamentary

[30] This term is used very loosely and here undoubtedly means India.

bill would not be able to be drawn up before Parliament's reopening at the end of the year. For I can hardly imagine that
the French ministry would be content with the simple promise
from London without seeing the bill in question. Since France
wishes to draw out the negotiations in view of events in India,
as Your Majesty deigns so well to observe, Spain does not wish
to press them further either, in the expectation of the reduction of
Gibraltar. The division in the English ministry, of which Count
de Vergennes confided to me some time ago his suspicion, and
which just now is coming into the open, is without doubt not
calculated to render England more formidable in the eyes of
her enemies but makes them firm, on the contrary, about listening
only to those proposals which they deem acceptable. At Versailles
they would be very pleased to hear the confirmation of the rumor,
which is widespread, that Admiral Howe will succeed Admiral
Keppel in the Admiralty, because that would remove the former
from the command of a fleet, and they believe him just as skilful
a general [*sic*] as he is a daring one.

61 : *Lusi to Frederick II**

LONDON, 23 July 1782

He [George III] is now persuaded that it is necessary to
renounce his sovereignty over America.

62 : *Von Thulemeier at the Hague to Frederick II**

THE HAGUE, 23 July 1782

In Holland they no longer deceive themselves about an early
peace. According to the news that has come to the Spanish minister and to Adams, the negotiations of Grenville at Paris have
not taken any firm form whatever. We are still being told of a

battle between Admiral Howe and the combined fleet, but this event hardly seems likely. The English general [*sic*] would compromise the last resource of the nation, if the outcome were unfavorable to him, while a victory scored over the enemy, unless contributing to the destruction of the naval forces of the House of Bourbon, would not end the war.

63 : *Goltz to Frederick II*

PARIS, 26 July 1782

Your Majesty deigns to remember what my very humble reports of the eighth and twelfth of this month contain about the new offer which the Imperial Courts have made to the Bourbon Courts about their mediation. It was on the twenty-third that France answered this. The note, delivered by Count de Vergennes to the ambassador of the Emperor [Joseph II of Austria] and to the Russian minister, and which these sent off by messenger for their courts, states in substance that the King acknowledges with a new sensibility the communication which the Emperor and the Tsarina of Russia have made to him about the British answer at the end of April and the reiterated offer of mediation; that His Majesty would always continue to have great concern for the last mentioned and to value exceedingly the desire, so much pursued by Their Imperial Majesties, to see a rapprochement between the belligerent powers; that sincerely animated by this same desire and in accord also with the wish of the Imperial Courts, the King had not believed himself able to refuse the direct negotiations which England had opened here by sending a person authorized by the most express powers; that the Court of London would without doubt not delay in revealing itself in this regard vis-à-vis the Imperial Courts, which would then be willing to communicate in this matter to the Bourbon Courts; that whatever might be the way to reach a suitable peace was a matter of indifference to the King, provided this salutary conclusion were reached. It would be very useless, Sire, for me to comment; Your Majesty knows perfectly the spirit in which this reply of France is conceived. From the bottom of their hearts they want to decline the mediation, but they want to make it clear to the Imperial Courts that it is England alone which now wants to avoid it. We will see what the Courts of Vienna and St. Petersburg make of this French answer along with that of London, and whether the latter will permit itself to be imposed on enough by them definitely to accept mediation, or whether it will continue to direct negotiations. In the meantime, since Grenville has been recalled to London, one other emissary, Oswald, who had been sent by Lord Shelburne to sound Doctor Franklin, has remained here.

64: *Goltz to Frederick II**

PARIS, 29 July 1782

As for Prince Kaunitz, it is very probable that his sagacity will take this reply at its true worth, and that while still affecting in public to believe that peace cannot be made except with mediation, he nevertheless knows in the bottom of his heart that the belligerent powers desire to pass it by. We must see whether after the receipt of this note of the twenty-third[31] the Imperial Courts will succeed in England, not only in having ministers named for a congress, but above all in getting a solid basis for negotiation put forward, and especially in having it preceded by independence pure and simple for America; for the nomination of English plenipotentiaries alone would not satisfy France nor, especially, Spain.

[31] A note by France in response to the offer of mediation.

65 : *Thulemeier to Frederick II* *

THE HAGUE, 30 July 1782

The change which recently took place in the British administration has not succeeded in discouraging the partisans that England has known how to keep friendly to her even yet in Holland. They doubt no longer but that the King of England will recover his prerogative and that the continuation of the American war will be among the projects of the new ministry.

66 : *Summary of the Negotiation at Paris**

(No date, but filed between despatches of 30 July and 1 August 1782)

The proposal made on the part of England, by Grenville to Vergennes, was:

That the King was ready to declare his intentions to concede complete independence to the thirteen American states and to cede to them New York, Charleston, and Georgia, including the town of Savannah, provided, however, that such a general and reciprocal restitution, in each quarter of the globe, be carried out on the part of all the belligerent powers, as would restore things to the condition where the Treaty of Paris of 1769[32] had left them.

This basis should not, however, exclude any exchange of possession made to the mutual satisfaction of the parties concerned.

The answer of Vergennes was:

That France consents that the Treaty of Paris should be the basis of the negotiations, but with exceptions and changes:

1. New arrangements concerning the East Indies.

2. New stipulations relative to Africa.

3. A settlement fair and mutually useful with regard to the fishing off Newfoundland.

[32] Seventeen sixty-three was meant.

4. A commercial arrangement to the satisfaction of the two nations in Europe.

That matters of restitutions and compensations should not be discussed until the negotiations should be started. That England will without delay make such overtures to the powers and states involved in the war as she deems proper to set the negotiations in motion. That France does not wish to treat unless the interests of her allies shall be decided at the same time, be it jointly or separately.

67 : *Frederick II to Goltz*

POTSDAM, 2 August 1782

As to what the new English ministry will do, it is difficult to speculate without knowing the principles it proposes to follow. But if peace is made just the same, it could be the achievement of this winter and not that of the present campaign. The Spanish want to have Gibraltar, and the French think they have some advantages in the East Indies. We must, therefore, wait and see. In the meantime I pray to God.

68 : *Thulemeier to Frederick II**

THE HAGUE, 2 August 1782

The financial resources that Spain and the American Confederation find in this country under the auspices of France are not abundant, and several successive loans have been given up as soon as launched. Adams hardly realizes that the re-establishment of peace in America seems yet far off. He maintains that the population, far from having decreased since the rupture of the former colonies with the mother country, has increased. According to him the duration of the war matters more to the people in the country than to those in the cities.

69 : *Goltz to Frederick II*

PARIS, 2 August 1782

A rich resident of Jamaica named Vaughan has just arrived here from London; he has not yet seen Count de Vergennes, with whom he has asked for a conference. I hope to know soon whether it is simply on a matter of arranging details of commerce for the islands, or whether Lord Shelburne wants to employ this new emissary to continue the work of Grenville. The latter case would seem strange, because it would evince an earnest desire to offer peace while the prime minister will not hear of the unqualified independence for America, which France has so often reiterated her desire to see precede any negotiation of the general peace. The brilliant maneuver of Lord Howe has augmented the high opinion of his talents held at Versailles as much as it has caused pain there. After having made all his movements during the day of the twelfth, with twenty-three ships against forty, in such wise as to leave no doubt to Don Cordova that he felt very fortunate to gain the night for entering the Channel, and after the latter expected to pursue him there on the morrow, the English admiral profited by the darkness, and by the speed of his vessels, and changed his course, suddenly heading for Cape Clear. By taking up this position he seems without any doubt to have saved the merchant fleet from Jamaica, if, in accordance with the advice forwarded to it, it is taking the Ireland route. Meanwhile, as they dare hope in this quarter that this information may well not have reached it, that it will therefore sail directly toward the English Channel, the combined fleet does not want to discontinue its patrol of Ouessant[33] to follow the English admiral. If this

[33] Ouessant is an island off Brest, at the entrance to the Channel. An

prize slips away, the appearance of the allied fleet on the coast this year will have been as useless as in the preceding years.

70: *Frederick II to Lusi*

POTSDAM, 5 August 1782

In so far as I can foresee and predict what will happen, I am led to believe that France will only wait until the end of the siege of Gibraltar to reach an agreement with England. If the negotiations recommence in September, peace will undoubtedly be concluded in the course of the winter.

71: *Goltz to Frederick II*

PARIS, 5 August 1782

Your Majesty reproaches me for my silence on the effect which the change in the ministry in England after the death of the Marquis of Rockingham had on the French ministry. I have dared to mention it since the news has arrived here, and especially on the occasion of the recall of Grenville. At Versailles it is believed more and more that the new British ministry is not well composed, that there is little unanimity among its members, little confidence placed in each one of them by the King, and up to the present, at least, no settled plan for either the negotiations or the conduct of the war. If the French cabinet sees this with satisfaction, the return of Lord North would undoubtedly cause it pain; his talents are well appreciated here, especially by Count de Vergennes. It is foreseen that if he returned to the ministry he would make very good use of the groundwork done by the current administration on more than one point which formerly

---

indecisive naval battle between the French and English had occurred there in 1778.

he would not have touched, because of his own principles, those of his colleagues, and even those of the King, his master.

72: *Frederick II to Goltz*

POTSDAM, 5 August 1782

I received your despatch of the twenty-sixth of July. I am convinced the English will continue to discuss negotiations where you are to try to bring things to a peaceful state as soon as they can. It seems to me at the same time very probable that, the undertaking against Gibraltar once lost, the uproar new taxes cause in France, and the difficulty of finding the necessary sums, will oblige the French government to put more effort into the negotiations of the peace treaty, and that therefore it could well be made in the course of the next winter.

73: *Goltz to Frederick II*

PARIS, 9 August 1782

The Marquis [*sic*] de Vergennes came after the arrival of the new English negotiator, Fitzherbert. He had seen him the day before and assured me that if he did not have anything more definite to say afterwards, it was because in this first conference the new negotiator had advanced no further than Grenville. I asked him how he thought the new British ministry could accord the unlimited independence of America after contrary commitments had been made to the King of England and all the nation. The Marquis [*sic*] de Vergennes replied that he understood it no better, but that he thought he could predict that Lord Shelburne would not hold his place long, and perhaps his master had elevated him in order to dishonor him in the mind of the nation. Upon my asking whether he would be astonished if Lord North should come back to power, he replied that it would not surprise him, provided that ex-minister had the good will to return, but that undoubtedly he would realize the difficulty of the position of the First Lord of the Treasury at the moment of the future peace, since it would be necessary for him as Prime Minister to arrange the consolidated debt.   After this summary of my conversation with the Marquis [*sic*] de Vergennes, I take the liberty of coming to another point of which I have been advised.   Without waiting for the reply of the House of Bourbon of 23 July, the Imperial Courts have just reiterated their offers of mediation.   Prince Kaunitz said that the desire of England to make peace is not equivocal, nor her confidence in the good offices of the mediators; that if the House of Bourbon feels the same way, the moment for peacemaking has arrived; that during the course of this war circumstances have so complicated the interests of the powers that mediation is the only way to arrive at peace; that after mature consideration the Imperial Courts adjudge the English proposals to be entirely admissable, and that they have decided to come to a halt there.   As Count Mercy and [Prince] Baria-tinsky[34] have only acquitted themselves of this office just now, I cannot know yet what impression it has made at Versailles.

74: *Frederick II to Lusi*

POTSDAM, 12 August 1782

The proposals which the English have made to France, which you have just communicated to me, and the reply of the latter to said proposals have already reached me.   It does not seem to me that it will be impossible to make a general peace, but as the King

[34] The ambassadors to France of Austria and Russia respectively. Count Florimond-Claude Mercy-Argenteau became ambassador in 1766 and did not quit his post until 1790.   Through Marie Antoinette's old tutor, the Abbé de Vermond, who remained with her court, Mercy corresponded with the Queen of France.

of Spain[35] is extremely stubborn in his ideas, we must await the
outcome of the siege of Gibraltar and see whether this town will
be captured or freed.   This decision once accomplished, I see no
obstacle which could prevent general peace.   But then the great
difficulty will consist principally in bringing France and England
into accord as regard their possessions in the East Indies [*sic*].
It appears that this subject interests France even more than the
subject of America itself.   God knows what the ideas of France
are, but I presume that this is the principal obstacle which is
embarrassing them.   I must also admit that in view of the announced partiality of the Emperor [Joseph II of Austria] for
France, I strongly doubt that he has the least concern for the
interests of England, and these would surely be sacrificed to the
interests of France if they were entrusted to him.   At the present
time the Imperator [*sic*—Catherine II] of Russia lets herself be
led by all the insinuations of the Emperor, so that this situation
deserves the greatest attention on the part of England in order
not to sacrifice her interests entirely to the insidious "policy" of
Prince Kaunitz.   No one has as yet spoken to me of mediation,
as you say it is their intention to do, but if the belligerent parties
agree that I ought to be involved in it, I will willingly do it;
nevertheless, I say, the fate of Gibraltar must be decided, and
the town either lost or saved, in order to begin negotiations,
since at the moment the King of Spain entertains the greatest
hopes of acquiring it, and nobody has enough influence on him
to persuade him to enter into negotiations before that time.

75: *Lusi to Frederick II*

LONDON, 13 August 1782

    The papers tell us, although the government assures us of not
having any news, that the British troops have evacuated St.

[35] Charles III.

Augustine and Georgia, and that the Savannah garrison and two regiments from Charleston have already arrived at Jamaica, where Admiral Pigot, who has replaced Lord Rodney, will make preparations to undertake something against the enemy.

In spite of the assurance with which this news is announced, it is probable that it owes its origin to the orders which the British ministry had given General Carleton on his departure from here to evacuate all the places occupied by troops in the thirteen united provinces, and to withdraw to Halifax and Quebec, in case the Americans should want to accept the English proposals of peace.

But Congress not having wished to treat directly with the British general, it is to be presumed that this evacuation did not take place, unless the garrisons of Savannah and St. Augustine have despaired of being able to defend themselves against the operations of the enemy. Moreover, I do not want to give credence to any necessity for bringing troops to the islands, where nothing could be undertaken at this season. . . .[36]

Lord Grantham told me yesterday that Fitzherbert had arrived in Paris, that the Count de Vergennes received him very well and indicated a desire to continue the negotiations for peace directly, so these negotiations are not interrupted; it is feared, nevertheless, that the French seek to prolong matters in order to await the issue of the siege of Gibraltar and the successful outcome which they still hope to obtain by the campaign in the East Indies [*sic*].

76: *Frederick II to Lusi*

CROSSEN, 15 August 1782

I well understand that the difficulty of finding funds for the payment of interest on new loans must lead England to wish for peace, but I believe that this campaign will be over before a pre-

[36] The hurricane season.

cise settlement can be reached. There must be no power, however little enlightened concerning its interests, which does not distrust the Emperor, and the English have been grossly enough deceived by him to be careful. They would do well, therefore, to insist on this quadruple alliance[37] that has been considered, although I believe England is hardly any longer a power from whom one could obtain much aid.[38]

77: *Lusi to Frederick II**

LONDON, 16 August 1782

The government has received news of the evacuation of Savannah, and it is feared that it will be necessary to do the same at Charleston, since they doubt they will be able to maintain themselves there.

78: *Thulemeier to Frederick II**

THE HAGUE, 16 August 1782

There are reports here from Philadelphia which announce the tragic end of the English Captain Asgill, whom General Washington must have had executed as a reprisal.[39]

[37] Great Britain, Russia, Prussia, and Denmark.

[38] Frederick II was undoubtedly thinking of the financial aid Prussia received from Great Britain during the Seven Years' War and contrasting this with what he presumed the present straitened financial condition of the British to be.

[39] Asgill was spared. An American officer taken prisoner, Captain Huddy, had been murdered by a British officer, against whom no action was taken by the British. In reprisal, as was the custom then, nineteen-year-old Captain Asgill was threatened with execution. His mother sent a pathetic plea for her innocent son to Vergennes, who in turn added a diplomatic plea for leniency on 29 July 1782. Congress shortly took action, and on 13 November Washington wrote a letter to Asgill releasing him. Four days previously La Luzerne had informed Carleton of the decision.

79: *Goltz to Frederick II*

PARIS, 16 August 1782

I can add nothing new relative to Fitzherbert, unless it is that he has intimated the act for the independence of America will be passed without delay and receive the Great Seal. I believe that he received the reply that this event was yet to take place, and, furthermore, as Congress had already said, it would only provide what America's arms had already procured for herself a long time ago; but that the general peace depended on what England could agree about the claims of her enemies, and that it was upon that matter that overtures were expected, whether by direct means or by means of the Imperial Courts, whichever way being a matter of indifference to France.

80: *Frederick II to Lusi*

NEISSE, 22 August 1782

At this present time I see the English are obliged to make peace at any price, for the reason that they cannot find the funds to back the great and prodigious loans they have made, which consequently are very insecure; but the important thing is to see how the siege of Gibraltar will be decided, whether the Spanish will be obliged to raise it, or whether they will take the town, and what success armed force will have in the East Indies [*sic*], before we can know how peace is to be made with Spain and

---

See Jared Sparks, *The Diplomatic Correspondence of the Revolution* (Boston), IV (1829), 5; XI (1830), 105-108, 128-130, 133, 135-139; VI, 458; IV (1829), 5; Sparks, *Correspondence of the American Revolution, Letters to Washington* (Boston, 1853), III, 533; Francis Wharton, *Revolutionary Diplomatic Correspondence of the United States* (Washington, 1889), V, 447-448, 463, 501, 617, 634-635, 833-834, 870, 872; VI, 3, 65, 228.

France, for it appears that France principally turns her attention in the direction of the East Indies [*sic*].

81 : *Lusi to Frederick II*

LONDON, 23 August 1782

We have no important news here from the outside. Only they say that Admiral Pigot has detached twenty vessels for New York in order to observe the proceedings of Vaudreuil, who must have left with an equal force for the Chesapeake. It is believed that this detachment is intended as support for the Americans who are said to wish to undertake the siege of New York. Others suspect that the French are planning an expedition to the island of Newfoundland. But the latter opinion does not appear any more probable than the first. The Americans knowing that the English have resolved to undertake nothing new against them and that New York will have to be returned to them sooner or later at the peace, it is not to be presumed that they would want to continue the hostilities needlessly. As for the supposed venture of the French against Newfoundland, it is very doubtful that they would have sufficient forces to assure a successful outcome. Consequently I have reason to believe that if the fleets have retired to America, it is for the purpose of guarding themselves from the hurricanes which usually head toward the islands during this season, and for the purposes of mutual observation.

82 : *Goltz to Frederick II*

PARIS, 23 August 1782

In the meantime, Fitzherbert having asked for a conference, Count de Vergennes arranged one for him, calling to it the minister of Spain and the American minister. The English emissary has announced there that the formal act of independence of America would be made public directly. He has proposed a cessation of hostilities and a prior agreement to restore things in the East Indies [*sic*] to the state they were in before the recent rupture. Count de Vergennes answered that first of all he had to wait for the recognition of independence; that once this was done the enemies of England would be able easily to decide on the suspension of hostilities. As for the article about India, he rejected that completely. Fitzherbert has sent a messenger, and awaits further instructions. It is a wonder, in view of the present state of affairs in the East Indies [*sic*], that the English cabinet has been able in the first place to make such a proposition, since they can scarcely fail to see any longer that it is on this side that France bids for success. The answer of Count de Vergennes to the article about the independence of America has been caused by what I have already had the honor to report, the mistrust that they have here in Lord Shelburne's manner of negotiation. As for the armistice, I am inclined to believe that even if this formal article of independence should come out right away, they would not press here for the armistice; France because of India, Spain because of Gibraltar.

83 : *Lusi to Frederick II*

LONDON, 27 August 1782

Since England has lost hope of making private arrangements, it is no longer doubtful, as I have had the honor of observing already in several of my earlier reports, that not being able to resist her numerous enemies any more, she sincerely desires to make a general peace. But the great difficulty in achieving that general peace is to know how to go about inducing her enemies to accept the conditions which she has proposed to them. The conditions that France would like to impose on her, which are

known to Your Majesty, are ruinous for England, and the ministry is not able to accept them without the risk of raising the
whole nation against its government. Thus if France continues
to insist on her exorbitant demands, England may see herself
forced, in spite of herself and against all hopes, to continue the
war. Meanwhile it is possible to hope, as Your Majesty deigns
to point out to me, that after the conclusion of the siege of Gibraltar and the East Indian operations the two parties will seek
out each other with more haste than they have shown up to
now.

84: *Frederick II to Lusi*†

BERLIN, 27 August 1782

I have received your despatch of the thirteenth of this month,
and its content not requiring any other answer, I will satisfy
myself with observing that it is apparently not wrongly that they
fear in London lest the French draw out the negotiations until
the outcome of the siege of Gibraltar and the end of the campaign.
The Court of Versailles, bound by its commitments with that
of Madrid, which holds the capture of that place so close to its
heart, hardly knows what else to do. But with this obstacle once
overcome, as it may well be to the advantage of the English if
Admiral Howe comes to the rescue in time, I am convinced
that they will think seriously of peace.

85: *Lusi to Frederick II*

LONDON, 3 September 1782

I have ascertained from good enough sources that the ministry assembled in council last Friday, and that its deliberations,
which lasted five hours, concerned the news brought by a courier

sent by Fitzherbert. No one has been able to tell me the result of that long conference, but if it is true that they were occupied there with matters of the negotiations begun at Paris, I would not have any great cause to show myself satisfied with the sincerity of Lord Grantham, who told me the day before that he had received no news of importance . . . . As for the direct negotiations, people who claim to be informed as to French affairs assure me that the Court of Versailles only seeks to beguile England, and that it would prefer to make peace by means of a congress, although Vaughan, the negotiator from Jamaica who accompanies Fitzherbert, bestirs himself a great deal around Franklin in order to make the negotiations succeed and measures up also to the confidence Lord Shelburne has placed in him, of which Your Majesty has been informed, without doubt, by other sources.

86: *Thulemeier to Frederick II**

THE HAGUE, 6 September 1782

The American Confederation has been able to raise only two million florins in Holland. Spain, after seeing a pecuniary negotiation of five million fail, reduced the loan to three, with extremely advantageous conditions: obvious proof of her urgent need. Although the Court of Versailles maintains that one hundred and sixty million livres, which the continuation of the war will require for the year 1783, will be deposited in the treasury of the French Monarch immediately, it is expected in other quarters that the third *vingtième* will bring in only forty million.

87: *Lusi to Frederick II*

LONDON, 6 September 1782

Lord Grantham, whom I asked if he did not have any news of the negotiations begun at Paris, did not deny the arrival of a

courier sent by Fitzherbert, assuring me, however, that he had
brought nothing of any particular interest or that could have
given rise to the long conference of the British cabinet, of which
I made mention in my last very humble despatch.   However, I
no longer find in this minister the same zeal to inform me of the
high points and the thread of the negotiation.   All that I have
been able to find out from him may be reduced to notions, of
which no one is ignorant, to the effect that France seeks to gain
time and draw out the affair until the end of the campaign.   This,
Sire, is one of the reasons why I remain in the same uncertainty
about the real sentiments of this court.

88: *Goltz to Frederick II*

PARIS, 6 September 1782

It has been learned that the convoy of troops and munitions,
destined both for India and for the Antilles, which for a long time
had been held up by unfavorable winds at the Isle of Aix, near
La Rochelle, finally set sail the second of this month.

89: *Goltz to Frederick II*

PARIS, 9 September 1782

As for the negotiating of Fitzherbert, I have reason to believe
that it is still as languishing as I last reported and will remain
that way until after the outcome of the siege of Gibraltar and the
campaign in the East Indies [*sic*].   They are still expecting direct
reports from de Dorives, although there is no doubt that French
arms were victorious in the month of March.   They regard this
advantage as all the more opportune, since it will have prepared
the Indian princes to listen favorably to the proposals of de Bussi,

to return to their own domains, throwing off the British yoke, and to trade freely with all the European powers.

90 : *Lusi to Frederick II*

LONDON, 13 September 1782

They have invented the news here, which they pretend to have received from America, that since the proposals made by England to Congress, the union among the United States[40] has begun to relax, and that certain of the provinces have already even refused to pay their quota for the prolongation of the war. But this has no foundation at all, the ministry has no intelligence from this quarter, and we are in general without news from abroad.

91 : *Thulemeier to Frederick II**

THE HAGUE, 17 September 1782

According to certain intelligence sent to the Russian minister by Simolin,[41] it seems that the hopes of an impending peace sustain themselves but feebly in London, to the point that they despair of seeing the negotiations take on any shape in the course of the winter, that is to say, before the opening of the campaign of 1783. It is true that the English bonds suddenly went up, and this change is attributed, though rather vaguely, either to a resolution of the ministry to recognize formally the independence of America, or to the arrival of the expected full powers, authorizing Count Aranda[42] to begin negotiations for a future agreement with Fitz-herbert . . . . It is Adams whom they accuse of being the leader of a lively intrigue against the Prince [Stadhouder], but I do

[40] *États unis.*
[41] The Russian ambassador in Great Britain.
[42] Spanish ambassador to France.

not perceive in the person of this American minister enough address or intelligence to lead any faction.

92: *Frederick II to Lusi*†

BERLIN, 17 September 1782

I have not received any despatches from you in the last two mails. I expect that the next to come will inform me of the decision that the British Court will finally have taken either to aid or to abandon Gibraltar, the fate of which will doubtless very much influence the continuation of the war, or the peace negotiations, which may begin during the coming winter. I am reminded in that regard that the Court of France has declared to The Hague that when Brantzen, minister of the Republic, arrives in Paris, Fitzherbert will make overtures to him for peace between the Republic and England, which would seem to indicate that the Courts of Versailles and London are in agreement to continue direct negotiations for peace. The Court of Russia no longer applies as much energy to her mediation efforts, since the revolution which has taken place in the Crimea[43] gives her other preoccupations.

93: *Thulemeier to Frederick II**

THE HAGUE, 24 September 1782

The sending of Gérard[44] to London again made the English bonds go up, and numbers of Frenchmen, beguiled by the hope

[43] Russia consolidated her grip on the Crimea in 1783. Within the decade much territory on the Black Sea was seized from Turkey.

[44] Samuel F. Bemis on p. 23 in his *Diplomacy of the American Revolution* (New York: Appleton-Century, 1935) explains a point that has been confused. Joseph Mathias Gérard de Rayneval, the emissary to London, was the younger brother of Conrad Alexandre Gérard, French minister to the Continental Congress.

of peace, made considerable purchases, even in the capital of England itself. It has been claimed that this mission was motivated by the desire of the French ministry to establish the independence of America as a preliminary condition, and the desire to negotiate it directly, while Count [*sic*] Shelburne, far from subscribing to this condition, is of the opinion that his nation ought not to grant it except as compensation for the British possessions captured by French arms in the West Indies. I have been assured that the King of England has shown anew that he will lend himself to this concession only with the greatest repugnance. As for the movements in favor of the mother country manifested in interior New England, which the ministry is following with so much complacency, it appears that as a matter of fact there does exist some discontent occasioned by rather high taxes and forced enlistments, but that this agitation is not great enough to produce a revolution in favor of England.

94: *Lusi to Frederick II*

LONDON, 24 September 1782

The news from America has nothing to say about the arrangement whereby it was supposed the colonies would make a separate peace with England.

95: *Frederick II to Lusi*†

BERLIN, 25 September 1782

I have finally received your two despatches of the third and the sixth of September, by which I see the uncertainty in which you find yourself about the true sentiments of the British ministry as regards us. If Lord Grantham explained to you no more clearly about the negotiation of peace than about the triple alliance, it may well be that this minister has informed you rightly in saying that he still did not have any precise notion about it. They have even written to me from Paris that Count de Vergennes has made Fitzherbert feel that it would be expedient for all parties to put off the negotiations to the end of this campaign, which appears to me very likely, and I believe that the French Court would still prefer to negotiate directly with England, although it pretends not to be opposed to the mediation of a congress, in order not to offend the two Imperial Courts.

96: *Goltz to Frederick II*

PARIS, 26 September 1782

Your most gracious direct order of the twelfth and the *rescrit* of the fourteenth of this month have come to me. Your Majesty has the goodness to speak to me in the first about the readiness with which the Bourbon Courts would set aside the offers of mediation. Likewise, indeed, they are not in too much of a hurry to answer the declaration of the Court of Vienna at the start of August. The accustomed slowness of the Court of Madrid is very convenient for the one here, on this particular point, although on many others they have often wished to see it come more promptly to a decision than it does. While they avoid the mediators, they want to give stability to the direct negotiations. Since Fitzherbert, although avowing daily the ardent desire of the court to make peace, does not yet state proposals which would really guarantee this desire, I believe that Rayneval has gone to London to press the British ministry to be more open, at the same time declaring to it that otherwise the Bourbon Courts will no longer be able to believe in the sincerity of His Britannic Majesty's desire for peace. This opinion about the mission of Rayneval seems the most likely to me; but additionally I have just learned it from a person connected with several members of the cabinet; this person added that this moment, when the reduction of Gibraltar is expected, would appear at Versailles more suitable than any other to make the London cabinet explain itself clearly, because with the fate of this place once decided, whether by having taken it or by having lost it, one would not want to lose an instant in detaching considerable forces to the Antilles, in event the war should continue.

97 : *Thulemeier to Frederick II**

THE HAGUE, 27 September 1782

The commercial treaty[45] between the American Confederation and the Estates General, which has so long been under discussion, has finally been put in order, and the small points of difficulty which were contested with Adams have now been smoothed out. If this treaty is not yet established with his required signature, the delay must be attributed to the innumerable formalities which the nature of this government requires.

98 : *Goltz to Frederick II*

PARIS, 29 September 1782

The desire [on the part of France to negotiate directly with England] for this liberty must necessarily increase after the reverses at Gibraltar. This event is too recently known for me to estimate the degree of the impression made on the French cabinet with regard to the peace. On the other hand it is well to wait and see to what degree it will have put new life into the Court

[45] A treaty of amity and commerce was signed 8 October 1782 at The Hague. See *Treaties and Other International Acts of The United States of America,* ed. Hunter Miller (Washington: Government Printing Office, 1931), II, 59.

of London and what will be their language now in the negotiations. Meanwhile, as for the sending of Rayneval to London,
I am reminded of the following account, which, however, I do
not wish to guarantee will be completely new to you; the source
from which I have taken it is sometimes rather good. On the
departure of Count de Grasse from London, Lord Shelburne
is supposed to have charged that admiral on behalf of His
Britannic Majesty to say to His Most Christian Majesty in
person that for the good of humanity His Britannic Majesty
would perhaps be able to consent to sacrifices, as soon as he
should be perfectly apprised of the moderation of His Most
Christian Majesty in this regard. Rayneval was sent to London
to obtain an explanation about the said sacrifices; he should
be returned by now. While it is not possible for me to determine
the impression that the catastrophe of Gibraltar has made on the
French ministry, I am sure that the King himself is very much
affected, not disheartened, but extremely dissatisfied with the
certainty with which this success is announced to him. It will
be quite another thing if, as is not impossible, Admiral Howe,
before entering the Straits, undertakes to burn Cadiz, which is
defenseless while the combined fleet lies at anchor in the Bay of
Algeciras.

As more and more the inconceivable inactivity of this fleet
makes itself felt, I believe I can see that Count de Vergennes will
prevail finally over the Ministry of Marine to make them use
Count d'Estaing, and that this admiral will leave in a few days
to go to this fleet. I still do not know whether he is to command
the whole fleet in Europe, or whether, and I believe this more
probable, he will go with a part of it to the Antilles and take
general command down there. What is to be regretted is that
he does not command the combined fleet at the present moment,
when the great superiority of forces, joined with the talents of
Count d'Estaing, would assure the advantage over Lord Howe;
instead of which, if an engagement took place today, the outcome

of the clash would be quite indecisive in spite of the fact that fifty-three vessels would meet thirty-six.

99: *Frederick II to Goltz**

POTSDAM, 30 September 1782

I almost have cause to doubt that the war will continue any longer than this year, since by and large France will have obtained just about what she wanted, that is the independence of the colonies, as well as some advantages gained in both the East and West Indies.

The preliminary Treaties

Following the news of the British success at Gibraltar in Sep-tember of 1782 the "desirable" articles lost all chance of attain-ment. Indeed the question of what would be done about the Loyalists and the debts owed to British subjects now assumed considerable proportions. Shelburne's ministry also threw into question the American claims to fish on the desired Newfound-land banks. Moreover, the Canadian boundary became a bargain-ing point, and the British considered claiming territory as far south as the Ohio to salvage what they could for the Empire and for compensation to the Loyalists. The American negotia-tors at this juncture gave up in their efforts for the Nipissing line, which would have given what is now Ontario to America by establishing a boundary drawn from the southernmost corner of Lake Nipissing to the source of the Mississippi. Instead they talked of both the present river and lake line and a proposed ex-tension of the forty-fifth parallel, from the Connecticut west to the Mississippi. The former was accepted as the boundary in the North, the Mississippi in the West, and in the South the thirty-first parallel and the St. Mary's River.

John Jay, in his fear of Bourbon projects, had proposed terms that would promote Anglo-American friendship. He sought reciprocally free terms for British and American navigation and trade. However, the only one of these terms which was pre-served in the preliminary treaty of 30 November 1782 was free navigation of the Mississippi. Nothing came of his hopes for mutual trade concessions. Partly as a result of his fear of the Spanish in Florida, a secret extra article was signed to the effect that if indeed the British got possession of Florida, the boundary would be moved northward nearly a degree and one half. Since the Spanish kept Florida, this clause did not take territory from America or give the Confederation a strong neighbor in the South.

Although the British negotiators went out of their way to talk a good deal about that unfortunate group, the Loyalists, only an empty recommendation by the Congress to the states was to be made. The American "liberty" to fish on the Newfoundland banks was granted, from which point much future wrangling was to develop. Franklin's "desirable" article about compensation for damage to American property was forgotten, and "creditors on either side" were to find "no lawful impediment" in the way of the collection of legally contracted debts. No confiscations or prosecutions were to be made, no future military seizure of territory would be valid, and the British troops were to be withdrawn, though the "convenient speed" stipulated by article seven permitted the British to stay in the West until the 1790's. Most significantly, however, the independence of the United States was pronounced.

This preliminary treaty, signed 30 November 1782 by Oswald for the British, and by Adams, Franklin, Jay, and Laurens for the Americans, was not to go into effect until the Franco-British preliminary treaty was signed. Although the American treaty was only conditional to the one between France and Great Britain, the mode and spirit of its conclusion showed that America was remarkably independent of France in diplomacy.

The preliminary treaty between France and Great Britain was signed 20 January 1783. The siege of Gibraltar was abandoned, and the British continued to hold this place, greatly to Frederick's admiration. Although France had fought for this great objective of Spain, she gave up the struggle for Gibraltar more readily than did her Bourbon ally. Since it had already

become clear that Great Britain would in any case consent to
a cession of Gibraltar only in exchange for other territory, some
knotty negotiations involving the Caribbean were avoided by
the British defense of Gibraltar. Spain, for her part, kept both
the Floridas, which she had seized during the war, and also Mi-
norca. The French took the island of Tobago, but they had to
hand back to the British all else they had taken in the Caribbean,
including Dominica and St. Christopher. The tiny islands of
St. Pierre and Miquelon were given to France in connection with
the fishing settlements. In Africa the British lost only their grip
on the Senegal River. In Central America limits were placed
upon their Honduran woodcutting. They maintained their favor-
able position in India. Except in North America, the changes
since the great British triumphs of 1763, when imperial heights
had been reached, were not great. Nevertheless, American inde-
pendence considerably impaired British preponderance. Although
Frederick was quick to observe how many of their losses the
British had recouped, he did not fail to regard the loss of the
thirteen continental North American colonies as a major imperial
blow.

100: *Lusi to Frederick II*

LONDON, 1 OCTOBER 1782

I have received your gracious *rescrit* of the sixth of September by which Your Majesty deigned to tell me that Brantzen had
been informed by the French minister at The Hague that upon
his arrival at Paris Fitzherbert would make overtures to him
about peace. This news confirms me in the suspicion that was
entertained here that the French court had sent negotiators to
London to smooth out the difficulties which block the negotiation
of the peace. Meanwhile, the British ministers keep, on this
subject, a most impenetrable secrecy to avoid the questions that

people would not fail to put to them.   Finally, they have not held a conference with the foreign ministers, and they avoid meeting them on all occasions.   Thus it only remains for you to make conjectures from hearsay with regard to that subject.   It is known, for example, that Lord Shelburne is often in conference with Lord Grantham, and that the latter, who is very busy, is aided in his work by General Yorke, his uncle.   They also say that the French negotiators have had several conferences with the English ministers about the independence of America.   Indisputably this is the means by which the negotiations must be begun, but it is also a point which all the English ministers cannot grant without the consent of Parliament, since according to the fundamental laws of the realm the King cannot part with any portion of his domains without the sanction of the legislative body of the nation.   Thus, from all appearances it will be necessary to go slowly in this business until the reopening of Parliament. If in the meantime they should want to come to an agreement on affairs of the East Indies and Newfoundland fishing, they could be taking a long step towards the peace, because this will be perhaps the most difficult point and the touchstone by which it will be seen whether there is mutually a sincere desire for the return of peace.   But it is probable, as I have already had the honor to call to the attention of Your Majesty in my last letter, that the English will try to draw things out in order to see the turn that new troubles in the Orient will take.

101: *Lusi to Frederick II*

LONDON, 4 October 1782

In spite of my scrutiny I have not been able to find out what the French negotiators have done here.   The general ignorance here on this subject makes me believe that this is the business of only one part of the English ministry.   The secrecy with which

Lord Shelburne deems it fitting to guard the proposals made by these emissaries, makes one suspect they have been very vague and that nothing has been decided, because in the opposite case he would not have failed to disseminate these to the public in order to encourage the nation by the hope of an early peace, which it ardently desires. I wanted to sound Lord Grantham on all this, citing to him the news which the papers mention and congratulating him on being well on his way toward re-establishing peace. He did not deny that France had sent negotiators, but also he did not confirm anything for me and simply assured me that as soon as there should be the least probability of a settlement Your Majesty would be one of the first to whom he would communicate the news, but that up to the present the direct negotiations were hardly developed and the two mediating courts had not taken any new step since the verbal intimation of which he had informed me two months ago. All that I have just explained only serves to confirm what I have already had the honor to tell Your Majesty in my last very humble despatches, that is to say, that they will await the outcome of the campaign and the denouement of the scene which is opening in the East.

102 : *Frederick II to Goltz*

POTSDAM, 10 October 1782

The siege of Gibraltar and its continuation is almost like trying to jump over the moon, but it is possible, nevertheless, that the obstinacy and the blind pertinacity of the King of Spain will oblige his soldiers to continue this siege and cool their heels uselessly before this place, as well as render entirely useless as large a fleet as the combined French and Spanish, of which good use could be made elsewhere. But in a government where caprice prevails over wisdom it is not astonishing to see incongruous things like this, which no sensible people would approve.

103: *Frederick II to Lusi*†

BERLIN, 12 October 1782

The notification you gave me of the arrival of a French negotiator can only mean the arrival of Rayneval, chief official in
the bureau of foreign affairs, who has, in fact, been sent to London, as I have told you, and who has already returned.   Perhaps
you will find the means of learning what was the motive of that
secret mission.   There are people who claim that its principal
purpose was to obtain explanations and some kind of assurance
of the recognition of the independence of America.   One sure
thing is that since the return of that emissary the conferences for
peace have taken on a little renewed vigor, and that one of them
took place 29 September at Franklin's place at Passy.

104: *Lusi to Frederick II*

LONDON, 13 October 1782

Nothing has since been heard about the negotiations of Rayneval, except what I have had the honor to tell Your Majesty in
my last very humble report.   Things will probably remain this
way until the end of the present campaign, although the refusal
of England to explain herself separately on one point, however
reasonable she may appear, could well deadlock the direct negotiations and make both parties look on the intervention of mediators as useful and even necessary.

105: *Goltz to Frederick II*

PARIS, 18 October 1782

The circumspection and the protestations of the French ministry to the Court of Vienna increase day by day.   I cannot refrain

from bringing to the eyes of Your Majesty the new proof which I have just received, and which I am sending in the envelope of de Rougemont. Count de Vergennes read a reasoned memoir in the council, in which he examined and discussed the reasons why France might be suspicious of the mediation of the two Imperial Courts; for one, the Court of Vienna would find in the continuation of the war stability for her Flemish commerce, and the other, Russia, would find the duration of the armed association ruinous for the commerce of the South. This minister finished by observing that being aware of the considerations that the two courts merited, particularly that of Vienna, he believed he could satisfy them by keeping them more or less informed of the state and progress of the negotiations. This line of action, the minister added, is so much the more necessary, since it will serve to keep the confidence of the Emperor and somewhat counteract the effect of the silence with which the Bourbon Courts received his last offer of mediation. This opinion met with no opposition in the council; it is, indeed, to be presumed that it was soon afterwards put into action, for it has been noticed that the ambassador from Vienna has more frequent conferences at Versailles than in the past. However adroit this step may be, it is hard to believe that it has lulled Count Mercy to the point of making him forget that Rayneval was secretly sent to London to agree upon a direct negotiation. If the Court [of Vienna] profits skilfully from these adventures, it will nonetheless keep its resentment at having seen its mediation eluded, if it should come about that the belligerent courts some time or other fall again into the hands of the mediators. Meanwhile, the peace conferences continue with a great deal of warmth. If I am correctly informed, the preliminaries consist of the following articles: independence will not be expressly pronounced by England in the treaty; but she will recognize the deputation of Congress as ministers of an independent power. East Indian affairs will be left undetermined until more reliable information is received.

Gibraltar will belong to whichever of the two powers finds itself in possession of it at the time the peace is signed. Finally, some exchanges in the islands will combine and compensate the interests of France and England.

106: *Goltz to Frederick II*

PARIS, 21 October 1782

The very gracious immediate order of the seventh and the *rescrit* of the eighth of this month have been delivered to me. As Your Majesty has the goodness to tell me, the burning of the floating batteries[1] at Gibraltar indeed fulfilled Your Majesty's prediction about the siege. I think, more and more, that they would easily have been consoled at Versailles for this catastrophe if it had disposed His Catholic Majesty to abandon the enterprise and to employ the same forces elsewhere; but, on the contrary, this monarch seems more determined than ever to persevere, and his father confessor confirms him in it, whether in good faith or to ingratiate himself. After the King of Spain had indicated to the Count of Artois that he wanted to see him remain at the siege because his departure would make Europe think the besiegers themselves did not hope for a prompt success, one should be astonished at the departure of that prince . . . . About the current mission of Rayneval at London, I can add today the following detail: Count de Vergennes had read to the council a memorandum on the dangers of committing their interests to mediators, who, even if one supposed them perfectly impartial, would like, at the least, each to retain an advantage from their good offices. He said that this inconvenience could be avoided by sending a trustworthy man to reiterate to the King of England the fact that the French share his desire to negotiate directly, and above all to make him see that the full recognition of American inde-

---

[1] Used by the combined fleet against the British.

pendence, on which Fitzherbert never pronounced anything positive, is an essential first step. I have been assured that the mission of Rayneval to Lord Shelburne procured for Oswald, who is here to treat with America, only an authorization from His Britannic Majesty to treat with Franklin as Minister of the United States.[2] Since Rayneval's return, Fitzherbert's conferences with all the ministers of the powers which are enemies of England have begun to come to life again, as I have already had the honor to state, but according to quite certain indications, I can only believe that the uncertainty about India forms the principal obstacle of the negotiations; that the Court of London is known to be much better informed than they are here; that its silence causes one to suppose that France has gained advantages but that, not knowing their extent here, they are afraid of losing these advantages entirely or in part if they come to an understanding with the enemy at this time. I have noticed that they make no secret here of the fact that if this ignorance in respect to India lasts until next year and the negotiations have not taken shape by that time, another campaign is likely. Regarding Spain, I have reason to believe that she is still demanding Gibraltar, not as a trading point in the negotiation, but as a condition without which His Catholic Majesty will not listen to any other. I may recall here that Count de Vergennes mentioned to me more than once that he considered the conservation of Minorca much more important than the conquest of Gibraltar, but that Spain as well as England set more store by Gibraltar, of the two, for reasons of prestige. At the moment of his departure Count d'Estaing was held over to receive some new instructions. Before proceeding to Cadiz, he will go to the Court

[2] Oswald's commission was altered in the latter part of September. Though it remained somewhat ambiguous, it now satisfied Jay, and it was because of American suspicion that it was changed. This delayed the conclusion of the preliminary treaty until after the defense of Gibraltar, which may not have been to the American advantage. See Bemis, *Diplomacy of the American Revolution*, pp. 211-227.

of Spain to obtain His Catholic Majesty's latest orders relating to the part of the combined fleets with which he will travel to the Antilles. There was in the council a very lively attack by the Minister of Finances against the Minister of Marine,[3] who is spending fifteen million a month, which the former considered to exceed the needs. Neither of the two is too sure of his post; however, I would not be surprised to see them both remain for the present.

107 : *Lusi to Frederick II*

LONDON, 22 October 1782

In the last conference that I had with Lord Grantham, I let him know that Your Majesty was informed of the reasons that had prevented Harris[4] from following up at St. Petersburg the questions of the projected alliance and of the intervention of Your Majesty in the mediation for the peace. He answered me by saying that he was charmed to hear that a true report on that subject had been made to Your Majesty, all the more as he had feared that the silence of the English envoy would be interpreted as a sign of indifference on the part of his court which could have given rise to unfounded mistrust, since the English ministry is ever of the same disposition and will continue to demonstrate the same confidence toward Your Majesty in communicating all that takes place relative to the negotiation of a peace. He next told me that the two imperial ministers had made new solicitations to him concerning the mediation of their courts, but that he had seen that it was on their own initiative and not on orders received from their sovereigns that they had taken this step. Since this last conference he has held a special meeting at Lord Shelburne's place, the subject of which must have been

[3] Fleury and de Castries respectively.
[4] British ambassador to Russia.

the despatches that have come from Paris. Although the subject of this meeting is not yet known, a favorable sign for the continuation of the direct negotiations can meanwhile be inferred from it, and in effect if the belligerent powers only succeed in putting aside their mutual mistrust, they will be able to adjust their interests without the intervention of mediators.

108: *Frederick II to Lusi*†

BERLIN, 22 October 1782

According to what I hear from France[5] and Holland, the direct negotiation of a peace must be making progress since Rayneval has returned from London. At Paris itself they have a better opinion of the peaceful dispositions of the English ministry, and I am assured that they are almost in agreement on the independence of America and on the mutual restoration of the conquests which were made on both sides. I hope that Lord Grantham will be a little more open about this with you since the departure of your last despatches.

109: *Frederick II to Lusi*

POTSDAM, 24 October 1782

I still suppose that peace will depend in a large measure on the delivery of supplies to Gibraltar, and that when that place is sufficiently provisioned, the negotiation of peace will become a little more lively. I dare say at the same time that we will have peace this winter, because all the belligerent powers are close to

[5] In the 1881 copy of this letter, which is not reproduced in the photostats of the Prussian Archives, there occur in the margin opposite the first line the words ". . . *des nouvelles intéressants.*"

the end of their resources. The King of Spain needs money and can get none from Holland. The new *vingtième* France has imposed on the people is not bringing in half what was expected, because of the impotence of the provinces, and as one cannot make war without money, it is to be expected that the end of their resources will be an effective motive for the belligerent powers to want peace. Add to this that the most favorable moment to make peace, for all the powers, is the moment when their mediators are themselves occupied in affairs which take all their attention, and it is to be believed that they will seize upon this moment by mutual choice and come to agreement among themselves.

110: *Thulemeier to Frederick II**

THE HAGUE, 25 October 1782

I do not know whether it would be right for me to put any faith in some news received at The Hague according to which several of the colonies formerly British, differing with the four provinces composing New England about the means of rapprochement with Great Britain, listen more or less favorably to the propositions which have been made to them by that power.

111: *Lusi to Frederick II*

LONDON, 25 October 1782

It would even seem that the meeting held at Lord Shelburne's place, which I had the honor to mention in my last very humble despatch, if indeed it did concern the matters of the negotiation of the peace, did not at any rate advance them very far, and to judge from what I have been able to understand from Lord

Grantham, the difficulties remain the same as before. From all appearances it will be necessary to have still more *pourparlers* and to hold more conferences before they will be able to take a decisive step to bring together the differing parties in such a manner as to reconcile the interests of the enemies of Great Britain with those of England, who, for her part, will try naturally to obtain her peace at the best possible price.

112: *Goltz to Frederick II*

PARIS, 25 October 1782

The ship of the line, the *Sceptre,* with two frigates, detached by the Marquis de Vaudreuil for Hudson Bay, successfully fulfilled its mission. De la Perouse, captain of this vessel, destroyed the small forts which protected the fur traders' warehouses; these were richly filled at the time; each soldier received thereby about fifteen hundred livres. On 10 September the Marquis de Vaudreuil set sail for Boston with thirteen ships of the line. The *Sceptre* not yet having returned, the Americans willingly furnished everything the squadron needed to reprovision; nevertheless they did not think they would finish before a month or six weeks, which would bring it to the end of this month; then they will probably return to the Antilles. At this same time, 10 September, the English fleet was cruising off New York, twenty-three ships strong according to some reports, twenty-eight according to others, under the orders of Admiral Pigot.

113: *Frederick II to Lusi†*

BERLIN, 26 October 1782

I have finally received your despatches of the first, the fourth, and the eighth of October, by which I see that at their sending no one in England had any precise news of what happened in the East Indies or at Gibraltar, or of the operations of the great English fleet, and that the British ministry keeps a profound secrecy about the peace negotiations, which undeniably have been undertaken by commissioners sent by both sides. I have already informed you by my last instructions that according to letters I received from Paris and The Hague, people discuss this in a manner that allows no doubt as to the progress of these negotiations. I am assured that the return of Rayneval has brought about the promise, which was mutually made, to let the mediation drop and to hold to direct negotiations. I have even been told that there has been agreement on certain preliminaries, according to which affairs in the East Indies would remain *in statu quo,* Gibraltar would go to that one of the two powers which has possession at the time of the signing of the peace, and hostilities in the Antilles would cease. I do not depend on the exact truth of that view. One has, however, reason to believe that the two parties will busy themselves more seriously with peace than in the past and are only waiting for the end of the campaign to finish the peace treaty. It seems that the independence of America cannot be an obstacle any more, having been granted in a certain way in the last meeting of Parliament, and the nation having even obliged the King of England to do this by the expulsion of the previous ministry.

114: *Frederick II to Lusi*

POTSDAM, 28 October 1782

The main thing to hope for meanwhile is that the peace will be concluded. According to my news from France it looks very much as though it may happen this winter. Nevertheless, I learn that Gibraltar will perhaps cause some difficulty, because they say the King of Spain is marvelously stubborn about this conquest, and perhaps will refuse to abandon it. But the great need of France for money for the war, the great need of the American colonies to hold their army together, and the great need of the King of Spain to have money, which he will not be able to repay, will be, apparently, invincible orators which will oblige the powers to make peace.

115: *Frederick II to Lusi*†

BERLIN, 29 October 1782

I have received your despatch of 11 October[6] by which I see that the British ministry still makes a mystery of the points on which it has negotiated with Rayneval. However, what Lord Grantham told you would seem to me to be true enough, since it occurs to me that the French ministry seems to be assured by the report of that emissary of the sincere dispositions of the British ministry for the re-establishment of peace, it being incredible, besides, that in such a course and in such a short time they would have been able to get to the bottom of the matter. One also can suppose that the peace negotiations will become more serious after the outcome of the present campaign has been determined, with regard to Gibraltar as well as for the East Indies [*sic*], and that even the re-establishment of peace will be reached during the course of the winter, especially if the balance among the belligerent powers remains nearly as it is at the present moment.

[6] Frederick must also have had Lusi's despatch of 4 October in mind; this letter appears above.

116: *Frederick II to Lusi*

POTSDAM, 31 October 1782

The news the English have just received from the East Indies [*sic*] according to your despatch of the fifteenth of this month is very good news for them. If they had taken it into account, it would certainly have influenced the conditions of peace very much. At the present we must wait to see how the fate of Gibraltar will be decided. For my part, I still hope that peace can be made this winter, and I think it will be the most favorable turn of events for them to avoid mediations which would not possibly be advantageous for them. That is all I can write you in reply. I have just one more question to ask: can they still find, where you are, the means to make a campaign if necessity arises, and where could these means be found?

117: *Goltz to Frederick II*

PARIS, 1 November 1782

Your Majesty does me the favor of telling me that the pre-occupation of the two Imperial Courts with their projects[7] against the Turks renders them less eager to mediate between the belligerent powers. My very humble reports received subsequently inform you I noticed Count de Vergennes and the Spanish ambassador[8] had the same opinion. In fact, for a long time Russia has no longer spoken of it at all, and Austria very lackadaisically. Meanwhile, to soften their refusal of the Emperor's good offices, the French keep him informed of the direct negotiations. These last, or so it seems to me, are still hampered by the uncertainty

[7] These projects matured in 1786 when an invasion occurred. The forces of Joseph II seized Belgrade, but it was later relinquished with no Austrian gain. By 1792, however, the Russians had obtained the Dniester boundary with the Ottoman Empire.

[8] The Spanish ambassador to France was Aranda.

in which they find themselves here as to the present state of affairs in the East Indies [*sic*]. Another difficulty is the resolution of the King of Spain not to commit Gibraltar to the negotiation, but to demand a promise for its cession before negotiating on the other points. It is more than apparent that since Lord Howe has supplied this garrison and undoubtedly detached a reinforcement to the Antilles the same moment he returned to the [Atlantic] Ocean [from operations in the Mediterranean around Gibraltar], the Court of London will become harder to please in the negotiations. This reinforcement will be greatly in excess of that which the combined fleet has just sent there. The consequences of the unfortunate engagement of the Count de Grasse are to be feared during the coming winter. As it was solely because of the desires of Spain that the combined fleet was kept completely together in Europe instead of gaining superiority in the Antilles in time, they are that much more displeased that Don Cordova let Admiral Howe escape from the Mediterranean, despite a superiority of more than a fourth, instead of forcing that admiral to an engagement. They lost a ship of the line, and four others were extremely damaged, while Lord Howe did not lose a single ship's boat. I have not been able to see Count de Vergennes since this distressing news, but I am well persuaded of his grief. He loves his country ardently, longs for an honorable peace, and must have felt that a complete fiasco would not approach it so soon. The Duchess de Polignac[9] is the favorite of the Queen, but at the same time the King has much friendship for her, so that this new favor does not represent any increase in favor. However, this princess takes pains more assiduously than in the past to offer marks of respect to the monarch, who is sensible of it, obliging her about the conferring

[9] Despite the enmity of the court, Marie Antoinette stood by her favorite. The Polignacs, realizing their unpopularity, emigrated in July 1789. One son, Jules Auguste Armand, became the head of the last ministry of Charles X and was responsible for the measures causing the Revolution of 1830.

of favors, but not listening to her in affairs of state. Count de
Vergennes has succeeded in avoiding her influence so far.

118: *Lusi to Frederick II*

LONDON, 1 November 1782

As for the negotiations for peace, they are no further advanced
than before, and since the departure of Rayneval no step has
been made on the part of England that might hasten the settlement. The ministry is making every effort to find means of
giving parliamentary affairs a favorable turn, and the nation is
concerned with the siege of Gibraltar and the fleet destined to
revictual this place. It appears, however, that they will continue
here to treat for peace by means of direct negotiations, and that
one may no longer have the same confidence in the mediating
courts.

119: *Frederick II to Lusi†*

BERLIN, 2 November 1782

I see by your despatch of 15 October that they are reassured
in England about the state of affairs of the Company[10] in India
by the last news they have received; but it is believed in Paris
that the British government knows more about this, to its disadvantage, which it does not publish, and that this very uncertainty has influence on the negotiations for peace. However,
I am assured that in Paris the negotiations are very much more
lively since the return of Rayneval; that the King of England
is willing to give independence to America, and that he has even
sent full powers to Oswald to negotiate with Franklin as minister
of the United States of America. It has also been confirmed

[10] The English East India Company.

for me in the most definite way, that all the parties have agreed to treat directly without any mediator. It is a sure thing that their interests are the same in this respect, if they really want peace, and one may suppose that they will find themselves so disposed, if Gibraltar is held without any action too decisive and advantageous for one side or the other, a situation which ought to be resolved in a short time.

120: *Goltz to Frederick II*

PARIS, 4 November 1782

They feel sharply at Versailles the inconceivably shameful blunder of the combined fleet in allowing the enemy to escape from the Mediterranean Sea, but more than that they feel the consequences which can result from it by the great excess of reinforcements undoubtedly detached to the Antilles by Admiral Howe over those which are to go there from Cadiz. If anything could lessen the bitter woe of the French ministry, it would be to see the King of Spain finally give up the attempt on Gibraltar and then to engage this monarch to employ his land and sea forces in a more profitable manner. Admiral Howe, being rid of his convoy since issuing from the Straits, may arrive at any instant in the Channel.

121: *Thulemeier to Frederick II**

THE HAGUE, 5 November 1782

The self-styled patriotic party has once more obtained a signal satisfaction at the expense of the Prince Stadhouder. A certain Baron Capellen,[11] a zealous advocate of the enemies of Great

[11] For Capellen, foreign propaganda, and the political situation of the United Provinces see Bemis, *Diplomacy of the American Revolution*, pp. 116-120.

Britain and of the Stadhouderat, notorious for his relations with the American Congress, having been excluded since the year 1776 from the House of Nobles of Overyssel, has just recovered that prerogative, thanks to an extreme agitation which makes itself manifest among the populace . . . . It is to be presumed that the Americans again have great need of help from France, since so many successive attempts to raise money in the commercial cities of the United Provinces have produced but meager sums.

122: *Frederick II to Lusi*

POTSDAM, 7 November 1782

The greatest obstacle to peace is, I believe, the fact that the campaign is not yet entirely decided, and when the powers know what to count on at Gibraltar, another difficulty will be that involving the East Indies [*sic*].

123: *Goltz to Frederick II*

PARIS, 8 November 1782

As to the great work of the war, I have reason to believe that Count d'Estaing, who left last week, is charged with putting to account the confidence with which the King of Spain honored him on his first trip, to persuade His Catholic Majesty to abandon the enterprise of Gibraltar and use his forces elsewhere. This admiral has much to gain from the success of this negotiation, since then the King of Spain would be willing to grant whatever number of ships Count d'Estaing would want to go from Cadiz to the Antilles; but a misfortune which cannot now be remedied is the delay of this departure. It can scarcely be hoped that it could take place before the month of December, by which time the English reinforcements may have arrived at the Antilles, if, as is probable, Admiral Howe detached them in leaving the Mediterranean Sea. They do not attempt to hide at Versailles the great superiority in ships which the English will have over there for some months, but they do not seem to fear for the islands, because the enemies of France do not have landing forces superior to the garrisons, especially of Martinique, which is in condition to defend itself in every regard, and is governed by the Marquis de Bouillé, a distinguished officer. I do not know whether they have reason to be reassured regarding the other islands in case Admiral Pigot should bring the garrisons of the Carolinas.

124: *Frederick II to Lusi†*

BERLIN, 9 November 1782

I have received at the same time your two despatches of the twenty-second and the twenty-fifth of October in which I see that the present British ministry is not as disposed as the preceding one to let you know what is being discussed in the peace negotiations which are at the present being considered in Paris. It is true that the progress of these negotiations will still depend on [future] events and especially on the outcome of the present campaign, which is becoming very interesting, especially at Gibraltar. It will be known by now in England that Lord Howe entered the Mediterranean with all his fleet on the thirteenth of October and sent part of his convoy to Gibraltar, but that he was followed by the whole of the combined fleet, and that consequently there can be expected furious battles and decisive events, although the combined fleet suffered considerable losses through storms. The British fleet has naturally more to risk in case of defeat than the allies, and England would lose by such a loss its principal resource. The outcome of this crisis cannot be far off.

125: *Thulemeier to Frederick II**
(Enclosure)

Gazette de la Haye
MONDAY, 11 November 1782

Extract from a letter from Paris of 3 November.
"Mr. Adams, Minister Plenipotentiary of the Congress to the Republic of Holland, arrived here four days ago. He is residing with Mr. Ben. Franklin. It is said that the subject of his trip is as interesting as it is mysterious."

126: *Frederick II to Goltz*

POTSDAM, 11 November 1782

This is terrible news that you have just given me—that Lord Howe, after bringing supplies to Gibraltar, left the Mediterranean again without being intercepted by the combined fleets. This does not presage the early capture of Gibraltar. The English, on the contrary, will gain the advantage of being able to have a decided superiority in America, from which they will surely know how to profit all the more, since the obstinacy of the King of Spain in wanting to continue the siege of the place in question will still tie up a part of the Spanish fleet, which could be employed more advantageously in other quarters.

127: *Goltz to Frederick II*

PARIS, 11 November 1782

Nothing could be more true than what Your Majesty deigns to say to me, in your recent order herewith acknowledged, about the need of peace for all the powers. A new attack which the Minister of Finance has just made on the Minister of Marine in the council in the presence of the King, proves again what a sinkhole of expenditure that navy is at the present time. The English Chancellor of the Exchequer will be no less embarrassed soon, in arranging for the funds necessary for the approaching campaign. In spite of this very important consideration, it seems that the negotiations are not proceeding as smoothly as they appeared to be at first after the return of Rayneval. Since then there has even been a scene between Count de Vergennes and Fitzherbert, which could well set back the work which has been done. The latter made some sort of reproaches to the effect that the desire for peace announced by France was contradicted by the mission of Count d'Estaing, who is known to be personally antagonistic to England, which has for its part more than one complaint against him. Count de Vergennes actively resented these remarks and made no attempt to conceal how strange he found it that the Court of London could think of asking the reason for any choice whatsoever made by His Most Christian Majesty among his generals[*sic*], and that this question alone could render suspect its good faith in the desire to make peace.

128: *Lusi to Frederick II*

LONDON, 12 November 1782

As for the direct negotiation of peace, there is not the least sign that any progress is being made. They do not agree, as had been believed, on letting the mediation drop, nor on the cession of Gibraltar, and as concerns the independence of America, Lord Grantham told me that this question had not been discussed with Rayneval.

129 : *Frederick II to Lusi*

POTSDAM, 14 November 1782

You can say to the ministers of the court where you are that Admiral Howe and General Elliot,[12] commandant of Gibraltar, both deserve to have their statues erected in London, because they have achieved, both of them, everything one could have hoped and have placed England in the position to make a peace much less disadvantageous than hitherto; but that nevertheless the best course for them would be to treat for peace without the intervention of any mediators.

130 : *Goltz to Frederick II*

PARIS, 15 November 1782

The time when the current troubles will be over seems to be retreating. Since a little while back the conferences have become much less frequent. May I recall the scene between the Count de Vergennes and Fitzherbert on the subject of the departure of the Count d'Estaing. The success of the English at Gibraltar, the greater part of the campaign lost for France in the East Indies [*sic*], the superiority of the British naval forces in America must necessarily raise the hopes of the Cabinet of St. James and render its agent much less agreeable than he was at first. Your Majesty will deign to remember that after the return of Rayneval from London the promise of the British ministry to recognize the independence of America seemed positive. In fact, the Court of London had circulated analogous insinuations in America; today the letters from England make one suspect that one ought not to be astonished if at the return of Parliament they decide vigorously to renew the war against the colonies. If England

[12] General Elliot had been in command at Gibraltar when the siege began in 1779 and remained there through the siege.

becomes stiffer toward the Bourbon Courts, she will be even more so against Holland. That is how it looks to me at the present moment. Your Majesty will deign to believe in my attention to the further progress of this negotiation; it could well be broken off suddenly in the judgment of persons often well informed. Some gazettes begin to speak of an Irishman, Newenham, who has come to this court as an agent of his compatriots. I find myself obliged to pause for a moment on this matter. Newenham is personally very much discontented with the Court of London, and in his bad humor he has come to try to raise hopes at Versailles of an approaching thunderclap in Ireland. Although the Count de Vergennes listened to him several times, he is quite far from being convinced that the discontent in Ireland has reached so dangerous a state for the Court of London as Newenham has persuaded himself.

131: *Frederick II to Lusi†*

BERLIN, 16 November 1782

I am now curious to hear how the Court and the British nation will have taken an event so fortunate,[13] which must surpass their hopes; whether they will be moved to continue the war, or whether they will know how to profit from it rather by making a tolerable peace that much the sooner, which would indeed be the wiser course. One will be able to see about this by the continuation of the negotiations begun at Paris, and perhaps also by the address that the King will have made to Parliament in its next opening and by the proposals which he will make to that assembly. I do not doubt that you will give all the attention necessary for subjects so interesting, and you will try to inform me about all which happens in this regard.

[13] At this point a mark calls attention to the following words in the margin: "Howe has arrived to reprovision Gibraltar and has re-entered the ocean without the slightest loss."

132 : *Count von Nostitz in Madrid to Frederick II**

MADRID, 18 November 1782

The goals of Spain in America are most far-flung. They would like to drive the English from the Bay of Honduras, expel them from Florida, and draw a line from Cape San Antonio to the mouth of the Gulf of Mexico in order to be able to exercise complete despotism over navigation and commerce in these latitudes.[14] It is certain that if the English were reduced to this necessity, they would rather consent to cede Florida to the United States of America than to the Spaniards, and even France would perhaps prefer this arrangement to any other because of the freedom of commerce and navigation. It is very improbable that the operations, the conduct of which will be entrusted to Count d'Estaing, with powers as broad as those which France has granted him, would correspond to such vast projects. However that may be, the financial resources of Spain appear too exhausted to sustain war for long in spite of what the ministers have falsely announced to the Count of Artois in this regard. If the English, whose resources are no less exhausted, let themselves be intimidated by the wise and effective measures which the allied powers are on the point of taking, and if in consequence of these fears they make propositions, however little advantageous for Spain, it is not to be doubted that the latter would gain more in listening to them than in pursuing her point, more especially as the Americans, having obtained from England what they wanted, and not being bound to Spain by the same ties which unite them to France, could very well remain inactive. Having made a particular study of the position and commerce of the new states of America, I believed I perceived some advantage for the

[14] Cape San Antonio is the westernmost point in Cuba. The word "mouth" here is a translation of the original "embouchure." Presumably this line would run from the southern tip of Florida through Cape San Antonio, delimiting thus the Gulf of Mexico. On the Honduran coast, the British were particularly interested in woodcutting.

states of Your Majesty in making haste to contract trade relations with this new power.   The overtures which I obtained in this regard, appearing to me to relate to the department of Baron von Schulenburg, I am sending them to him by today's courier, and I merely observe here that the immensity of the profit to be made on freight, by a neutral power whose flag is as respected as that of Your Majesty, would at the present moment be a sufficient inducement for sending envoys.   One would by this means gain preference over other commercial nations relative to the Americans at the conclusion of peace.   But if one were really to seize upon this opportune moment, it would be necessary to have shipments of exports which the Prussian states could furnish to America standing ready and send them there without delay, in order to get ahead of the other countries.

133: *Goltz to Frederick II*

PARIS, 18 November 1782

After a conversation yesterday with a man well acquainted in the *bureaux,* I am more convinced than ever of the slowing down of the peace negotiations about which, several mails back, I had the honor to forewarn Your Majesty.   It is Spain which, after so poorly seconding France in the operations, today causes the greatest embarrassment to Count de Vergennes.   On the one hand, she insists upon standing by her demands in North America and upon the cession of Gibraltar.   On the other hand, she is not benevolently disposed to the Americans, much less so than France would like.   Today Count de Vergennes is feeling badly about the precipitateness of Count de Maurepas[15] in having recognized the independence of America without its having been equally

[15] This is a reference to the situation of the French ministry at the outbreak of the American revolution. Except for Turgot, all the ministers, including the central figure, Count de Maurepas, favored aiding the colonies.

recognized by Spain. It is the bad luck of this minister that precisely at this moment British arms appear to be having all the successes, with the result that the Court of London becomes harder for France to deal with while she is quietly expending every effort to gain the co-operation of Spain. The cession of Gibraltar, not because of what it is actually worth, but because of the importance the King of Spain attaches to it, will undoubtedly be one of the key questions. Count de Vergennes faces these two cruel alternatives: seeing the King of Spain withdraw from the game, or making a sorry peace. The King, who has been led to expect a good peace in the course of the winter, is beginning to show irritation towards the Count de Vergennes, who until now, of all his ministers, was the one His Majesty most distinguished by his confidence.

He sees himself thus by a chain of circumstances at the discretion of Spain, and despairs of being able to make a worthy peace for France. All that remains for him to hope is that Spain should want to continue the war and that Count d'Estaing should persuade the King of Spain to send the combined fleet, or at least the major part of it, to the Antilles, in order to place under the command of that admiral the greater number of forces in that area, and finally to undertake the capture of Jamaica. In the same conversation mention was made of what was said in the communication of 26 October about the alarm felt in the city of Amsterdam because the French commandants in the captured Dutch possessions[16] referred to themselves as governors of French colonies. I was assured that France is very far, at the present time, from any thought of keeping those possessions. As for the sending of the governor of Berbice[17] as a prisoner to Surinam, ordered by Kirsaint, it was merely sending him back to a competent tribunal and having him judged by his masters.

[16] A number of Dutch possessions had been taken by the British, who in turn lost them to the French.
[17] In Guiana.

134: *Thulemeier to Frederick II**

THE HAGUE, 19 November 1782

According to the news which has come from London lately, it appeared that certain members of the former ministry were being won over to those who make up the present administration by the offer of more or less lucrative posts, with the purpose of weakening the opposition forces, which, in fact, do seem very redoubtable. It will be the opinion in the first sessions of Parliament, both about American independence and about continuing the war with the House of Bourbon, that will decide the soundness of the negotiations for general peace still going on at Paris; a soundness which has appeared until now extremely doubtful.

135: *Lusi to Frederick II*

LONDON, 19 November 1782

Once the campaign is over, one may expect to see the belligerent powers negotiate for peace with more ardor than they have shown up to now, but to judge from the eagerness that has been shown mutually to seek a rapprochement, one would be tempted to believe that the negotiations are not ready to reach their fruition; at least one does not see that the Cabinet of St. James makes the least move towards forwarding them, and Lord Grantham, whom I believed I should sound on this point, answered me in a manner which leaves no doubt that for their part no real efforts will be made to hasten a settlement; moreover, the big preparations that are being made for the continuation of the war do not presage very peaceful sentiments, and the nation no longer seems as much inclined towards peace as it was last year. The late campaign, which was more glorious for Great Britain than for her enemies, has given birth to the hope that by pursuing the

war with vigor they will succeed in changing the appearance of
things, and those who have the most presumption do not despair
of being able yet to subject the American Confederation, or at
least to gain advantages great enough to counterbalance the loss
of the colonies.   The knowledge of the true situation of things
should without doubt dissipate such fantastic hopes as these in
the British cabinet, but it still is inclined towards war.

136: *Frederick II to Goltz*

POTSDAM, 21 November 1782

As for peace it depends without a doubt on the willingness of
the belligerent powers.   But it is strongly desired in all of Europe
because of the cruel restraint under which the commerce of all
nations languishes.   That, however, is no reason for these same
powers to come to an agreement.   I think they will have to be
given time to empty their money bags cleanly in order for peace
to come out of those depths, as from the box of Pandora, where,
after all the ills were outside, hope alone remained.   In general
I can tell you in regard to the Turks and the Russians that unless
something happens that cannot be foreseen at this moment, one
can count on it that the Tsarina will carry out her entire project.

137: *Goltz to Frederick II*

PARIS, 22 November 1782

In my last very humble report I spoke of the difficulties which
have unexpectedly arisen.   Now Rayneval has just been sent a
second time to London.[18]   Here is what I permit myself to think

[18] Rayneval had first been sent to London in September, when the
Spanish designs on the trans-Allegheny territory were being pushed.   On
his second trip on 15 November he was trying to arrange for the cession

of his mission: at his first return this emissary spoke of the assurances of Lord Shelburne of the recognition of the independence of America. From this moment the conference between the belligerent parties came to life here, but since then, not only is England less explicit about this recognition, but they fear here that at the coming reopening of Parliament the Court of London will take one of two courses, either to make a decision for the continuation of hostilities against the rebels or to accord them independence, but at the same time to attach the new power to England by treaties, and to continue the war that much more vigorously against their other enemies. I would therefore willingly believe that Rayneval has gone to try to obtain a categorical reply relative to America, so that in case of a refusal France could at once break off all negotiation. Count de Vergennes is personally concerned lest England bring about the rupture of the negotiations, since the King his master, being already dissatisfied by the turn affairs have taken, will easily lend an ear to the enemies of the minister, who will not fail to accuse him of being duped by England. I said above that the latter might accord independence while attaching the new nation to itself. A secretary[19] has just come from the French minister in America, despatched to give advice of the results of the British negotiations. La Luzerne[20] is urgently demanding a reinforcement of troops, money, and other necessities. The Marquis de Lafayette leaves from Brest soon with two regiments.

---

of Gibraltar in exchange for such compensation to the British in the Caribbean as Porto Rico. On his third trip shortly afterward he reported Shelburne's intention to keep Gibraltar but willingness to cede Minorca and the Floridas to Spain. This was the settlement. See Bemis, pp. 243-247.

[19] The secretary of the French legation in Philadelphia was Barbé-Marbois.

[20] La Luzerne, replacing Gérard in 1779, was the second French minister to the Congress.

138: *Lusi to Frederick II*

LONDON, 22 November 1782

If one is to judge the peaceful intentions of the British ministry by its eagerness to revive the negotiations at Paris and by the care that it takes to show this eagerness to the public, there would be nothing to expect but the conclusion of peace soon. In the space of two days three couriers have been sent to Fitzherbert, and rumors have been circulated that the negotiations have advanced considerably. Lord Grantham also has changed his manner of speaking and said to me that lately there have been some hopes of success, although the claims of the allies are yet of such nature as cannot be granted. But all these demonstrations deceive the great majority without being able to deceive those who are informed of the true manner of thinking of the King and Lord Shelburne. They claim that both are trying to find the funds necessary to continue the war, that they are resolved to risk one more campaign, and that they make the appearance of wanting peace for two reasons, the first: in order to raise the funds to facilitate for those involved in the loan of the present year the last payment which they have yet to make, which amounts to the sum of five millions, including the three and one-half millions which the bank has advanced to lenders and which would be settled at the same time. The second reason: in order to justify themselves in Parliament, where the opposition will not fail to accuse the ministry of having abandoned the plan of making peace, which had been laid out under the administration of the Marquis of Rockingham. As for raising funds, they have already attained their goal. They have increased by three and one-half per cent; it remains to be seen if they can persuade Parliament that the exorbitant demands of the enemies of Great Britain prevent the ministry from concluding the peace. While waiting, it seems that they still forever flatter themselves here that they see troubles developing in Germany which will bring a diversion to the forces of France.

139: *Frederick II to Lusi*

POTSDAM, 25 November 1782

I can indicate to you in general that it appears from my letters from France that many people there believe that the war could well continue through the coming year, because, they say, the English have raised their pretensions too high. I do not know what to say in regard to this. I am not informed as to whether they have offered new proposals or not. But if war goes on for another year, the belligerent parties on both sides will be so exhausted that they will not be able to gather strength to move for a long time.

140: *Goltz to Frederick II*

PARIS, 25 November 1782

My last very humble report concerned the new mission of Rayneval to London. My latest information confirms me in what I believed was the motive for this step. I have been assured that this negotiator is charged with summoning the Court of London to fulfil at once the promise, given last summer, to recognize the independence of America; that he is not to conceal the fact that Spain is much less disposed to peace than they are at Versailles; that he is even bearer of a copy of a letter from the King of France to the King of Spain asking him to insist less on the cession of Gibraltar and on the conservation of all Spain has acquired in this war with England. Finally that he may intimate that the lively and sincere desire of His Most Christian Majesty for peace could well dispose him to reinstate the situation in the two Indies at the point where it was before the rupture. If, as I believe, such is the commission of Rayneval, the recognition of the independence of America would render peace inevitable, unless the King of Spain should persevere for the cessions. The unfortunate battle of 12 April[21] in America and the campaign lost in the East Indies [*sic*] make Versailles now regard this independence of America as a price of peace, whereas last spring they envisaged it as secondary, and the principal objective for France was to crush the English in India and for the Spanish to conquer Jamaica.

141: *Lusi to Frederick II*

LONDON, 26 November 1782

Since the departure of the last post rumors of peace have been circulating here. It is known that Rayneval was at London a week, and that he left the twenty-fourth of this month with the latest resolutions of the cabinet of St. James. Parliament, which was supposed to hold its first session today, has been postponed until the fifth of December, and it is in the space of these eight days that the British ministry expects to have certainty as to whether peace can be concluded or whether it will be necessary to continue the war. Townshend[22] wrote a letter, which has been made public, to the Directors of the Bank, in which he said that the negotiations at Paris had progressed to the point where one will soon see whether the enemy wishes peace or not. All the other ministers openly speak in the same vein; but the conditions on which they wish to conclude their agreement are not divulged. Those who claim to be informed would have us believe that Great Britain, in her final offer, accords absolute independence

[21] The naval victory of Rodney in the Caribbean.

[22] Thomas Townshend, Secretary of State for home and colonial affairs in the Shelburne cabinet. Oswald was responsible to him; Fitzherbert was responsible to the Secretary of State for Foreign Affairs, Grantham.

to the United States of America, that she returns the establishments in the East Indies [*sic*] that France has lost there during this war, and allows her to keep Grenada, reserving the right to come to agreement later about the exchange of several islands in the West Indies. Spain will possess, they say, Gibraltar, Minorca, and western Florida, but she will give the English in exchange Porto Rico, to serve as a retreat for the American Loyalists.[23] Finally, the Dutch will repossess the establishments they have lost.

However that may be, it is very certain that Lord Shelburne made haste to advance the negotiations in order not to incur the reproach of the nation that he wishes to prolong the war; and since he has not yet taken the necessary steps to cover himself on this point against the criticism of the opposition, he thought it wise to postpone Parliament in order to gain the time which he absolutely needed to advance things to a point which he could justify before this assembly as not having altered the patriotic policy. In whatever way things are going at present, they cannot but be advantageous to Lord Shelburne, whether the allies require hard conditions from Great Britain, or whether they content themselves with the proposals that the latter has made them for the peace. In the first case the minister would present those conditions to Parliament and ask whether the nation wishes to buy peace at that price. If Parliament responds negatively, it thereby obliges itself to furnish the necessary appropriations and cannot impute to the minister the blame for allowing to fade away the hopes of peace that it has itself rejected. In the second case, if Parliament gives its consent to the proposals which have been made to France, it takes responsibility for the action and Lord Shelburne is shielded from the future recrimination which his enemies might make that he had concluded a peace which, in effect, no matter how it turned out could be neither advantageous nor

[23] This would have been along the lines proposed by Rayneval on his second trip.

glorious to the English nation. It remains to be seen whether France sincerely wants peace. In any case the English are very determined to add nothing to what they have offered, and the ministry will make every effort to continue the war with success if Parliament is dissatisfied with the concessions they are making to avoid its continuance.

142 : *Frederick II to Lusi†*

BERLIN, 26 November 1782

I have just received together your reports of the fifth, the eighth, and the twelfth of November, by which I see that the great and fortunate event which has just come to pass in the Mediterranean has not yet made any decided change either in the internal administration of England or in the peace making. It will show more effect, however, according to all indications, at the reconvening of Parliament, and it appears that the British government ought to profit by the present tolerable situation of its affairs by obtaining a peace settlement, however little advantageous it might be, for if the King of Spain once gave up the siege of Gibraltar, and the two Bourbon Courts joined their forces in America, it would be difficult for the English nation to resist them for any length of time and save Jamaica, a possession more valuable to England than any other, but difficult to defend.

143 : *Lusi to Frederick II*

LONDON, 29 November 1782

Meanwhile, the hope for peace is quite general here; at the same time it seems that the nation wishes for it more than it expects it, because the public funds[24] which are regarded as the thermometer which indicates the degree of confidence or fear of the nation are continually extended, and are not going up as much as one would have thought. As for the influence of Lord Bute in affairs, I have nothing to add to what I had the honor to report to Your Majesty in my very humble report of the seventeenth of this month, and as Lord Shelburne preferred to make all the advances for the peace rather than try to lay it to the former ministry, it is very certain that none of the partisans of Lord Bute will be employed, and that Lord Shelburne, sustaining himself by means of his efforts for peace, will continue to direct the King and the affairs of state.

144 : *Goltz to Frederick II*

PARIS, 29 November 1782

If he could hope for it, this minister [Vergennes] would probably not be displeased with the great occupation* the Tsarina of Russia, whose predeliction for England seems to increase every day, is going to undertake. Seen from the present standpoint here, Count de Vergennes must wish, in effect, that the two Imperial Courts would occupy themselves in their own behalf, provided success were not too rapid, for the sake both of the conduct of the war and of the peace negotiations, concerning which I think I can refer to my last very humble reports. If the performance of the combined fleet, both in its cruise last summer and later in the Mediterranean gives a poor idea of its commanders, they are worth even less than that according to what we learn from those who followed the Count d'Artois to the siege of Gibraltar. I am not ignorant of the fact that the

---

[24] The word was *"fonds,"* perhaps in the sense of bonds.

* The translation here is literal: the original reads *occupation.* The reference may be to the Russian occupation of the Crimea, which took place in 1783.

courtiers of Versailles have a rather grandiose opinion of their own talents, and that they are prone to have a low opinion of the talents of others; but they are in possession of so many facts relative to the Spanish generals that it would be impossible to misrepresent. On the subject of the mission of Count d'Estaing, I am led to believe even more than I was before that the principal purpose of it is to dissuade the King of Spain entirely from continuing the siege of Gibraltar, and to engage him to send the greater part of the combined fleet to the Antilles. But if, in hope of reconquering Jamaica, the monarch consents to this detachment, there is every reason to wager, in view of the delay of this fleet, which has done nothing, that Count d'Estaing will not be able to set sail until the new year. Your Majesty will already know that in the meantime Admiral Howe has detached eight ships for the Antilles, which may be there now, and is having Admiral Pigot stand in readiness, because he will certainly be careful to prevent the Spanish ships from joining the French, a combination which still never would be a sufficient force against the English. At Versailles they are in a great state of impatience concerning what took place at the reopening of the British Parliament, both about the question of peace and about the Americans. The conversations that Rayneval will have had since will put Count de Vergennes in a position to judge what he can expect from his emissary's sojourn in London, and that in less than five or six days.

145: *Goltz to Frederick II*

PARIS, 2 December 1782

From the first moment that they knew here of the postponement of the English Parliament, they predicted an early decision for peace or for continued war, because probably His Britannic Majesty only postponed the reopening to avoid the clash between the differing parties; but what gave credence indeed to this opinion was the arrival of Rayneval. After one day's stay at Versailles he left again for London. His Most Christian Majesty as well as Count de Vergennes looks pleased, which makes one think even more that the English reply brought by Rayneval considerably advanced the cause of peace. After a conversation with a man very well informed about the *bureaux* I can confirm the suspicion I had the honor of writing you, that the recognition of the independence of America by England will probably suffice to arrange the preliminaries with France. As for Spain, it will indeed be necessary to buy her off with Gibraltar. They would rather that she preferred Minorca, a place, in fact, more important; but His Catholic Majesty does not feel that way. This monarch is also still holding out for the retention of what he has conquered in Florida, but it is believed that he will be less determined if once he is assured of Gibraltar. If, in fact, the preliminaries are going to be signed right away, I will take the greatest pains to find out to what degree the return of peace will oblige the French ministry to turn its attention to the affairs of the Porte, although the weakened state in which the war has left the finances of the House of Bourbon must preclude its direct intervention in favor of the Turks.

146: *Frederick II to Lusi*†

BERLIN, 3 December 1782

I have already gone many mails without having any despatches from you, and I am so much the more impatient to receive some, since I expect to learn thereby the effect which the fortunate end of the campaign will have produced on the nation and the British government, and what policy the latter will follow at the opening of Parliament, whether for peace, or for the continuation of the war. According to my last letters from Paris they have not only resumed the packet boats between Dover and Calais, but the conferences are also continuing between the negotiators of the belligerent powers, and the Court of France has even sent Rayneval back to London, which appears to indicate that France wishes to pursue the negotiation of peace vigorously, and that she is trying to get around the obstacles to it. Perhaps, also, she wants to try to sound out the true feelings of the British government in the present session of Parliament.

147 : *Lusi to Frederick II*

LONDON, 6 December 1782

At the conclusion of the cabinet meeting which took place the day of the departure of my last very humble despatch, Townshend, the Secretary of State, wrote a letter to the Lord Mayor of London, to be made public, in which he informed him that a courier from Paris had just brought the news that the commissioners of His Britannic Majesty and those of the United States of America had signed, on the thirtieth of November, a provisional act which would be inserted in the treaty with France as soon as that should finally be completed. This news, although interesting, was altogether unexpected, because it was hoped to learn at least the entire result of the negotiations, and that is what made me determine not to communicate it to Your Majesty until I should be in a position to confirm its authenticity. That is what I have the honor to be able to do today. . . . [The Parliament assembled yesterday with the solemnities that are the custom on this occasion. From the throne the King gave a speech to the two Houses, of which I should have liked to send Your Majesty a translation; but time not permitting me to do this, I will content myself with giving an extract, from which I will leave out nothing essential.

[His Majesty began by making it known that he had followed the will of Parliament and of the nation in halting the hostilities in America, and that all the measures he had taken, both in Europe and in the new world, had no other goal but a complete reconciliation with the colonies.

["Finding that in order to arrive at this conclusion (these are the exact words of the address), it would be indispensable that I should avail myself of the full extent of power of which I am invested, I have not hesitated to avail myself of it, and I have offered to recognize the colonies, a free and independent state, by an article which should be inserted in the treaty of peace. This matter has been agreed upon in provisional articles which shall not have treaty force until a definitive peace is concluded with the French Court.

["In agreeing thus to the separation of the colonies from the British Empire, I have sacrificed all my personal considerations to the wish and opinion of the people; and I implore the Almighty, by the most fervent prayers, not to let Great Britain feel the misfortunes which can result from such a great dismemberment, and to preserve America from the calamities which formerly proved to the mother country how essential monarchy is to the enjoyment of lawful liberty. Religion, language, interests, and inclination can and, I hope, will form a bond of permanent union between the two lands. It is to that end that I, for my part, am particularly desirous of devoting all my attention."

[His Majesty, after praising the brave defense of the commandant of Gibraltar, the skill of the admiral who reprovisioned the place, the bravery of his armies in general, and the patriotic spirit of his subjects, who have given evidences of it, he said, which will do them honor in all ages and in all lands, thus continued his address:

["Having then shown to all the world, by deeds which may long serve to exemplify the spirit and the signal courage of my people, I believed that it would not be contrary to my dignity, and that it would even be in conformance with the regard that I ought to have for the life and the property of my brave subjects, to make clear my position in arriving at the terms of an honorable settlement with all the powers at war.

["I have the satisfaction of announcing to you that in this regard the negotiations are quite well advanced. The results will be communicated to you as soon as they are brought to a conclusion. I have every grounds for hoping and believing that in a little while I shall be in a position to inform you that they have ended in a peace, of which I flatter myself that you will have reason to approve the conditions.

["However, if in the dispositions of the belligerent powers an unexpected change should occur, which would deceive my hopes, I will put my trust in my Parliament and the spirit which animates my people, confident that they will approve the preparations I have deemed fitting to make, and that they will support me in the vigorous pursuit of the war."

[His Majesty next informed the House of Commons of the measures he had taken to economize in the expenditures of the army, of the savings he had introduced in those of the royal household, and the reforms he had instituted so that his expenses would no longer exceed his revenues.

["My debt, being somewhat larger than it was shown exactly in the record, and the reforms not having been able to take effect right away, I hope that you will look to the surplus; you are assured of repayment, as I have already promised, from my annual revenue."

[His Majesty recommended to the care of the House of Commons the American Loyalists, who have suffered by the war because of their attachment to the mother country; and he called attention to other questions concerning finances or internal administration of the realm. He ended by picturing India to his Parliament as a vast field where it can exercise its wisdom and foresight in settling matters in such a manner that the bonds which attach these Asiatic provinces to Great Britain may be a blessing to those lands; and where it can to take all suitable measures to inspire foreign nations, in respect to international commerce, with confidence in the probity, punctuality, and good order of the English government.

[The last point not being entirely clear, and there being no explanation of the kind of commerce His Majesty had in view, it will be necessary to see by the settlements Parliament will make on this subject what is in question. It is not yet known what impression this interesting address will make on the spirit of the nation, but the expression of thanks to the King has passed unanimously in the two Houses. Lord North and Lord Stormont[25] have seemed willing to oppose the measures of the ministry in the House of Lords, but they will find it difficult to make themselves a party of any weight. In the Commons Fox has declared he does not want to oppose the administration, so long as it follows the policy that has been adopted, but he has cried out against the cession of Gibraltar, which he believes to have been made to Spain.

[The address of the King proves clearly that Lord Shelburne, instead of having discredited the system of Lord Bute, was able to get the approval of His Majesty for his own. Nothing is more indicative of it than the solemn promise not to spend beyond his revenues and not to undertake anything without the approval of his people].[26] As for the negotiation of peace, it is quite generally believed here that it will not be concluded and that another campaign will be required to bring the warring parties to agreement. With the exception of a handful of commercial magnates, who desire the continuation of the war, all the rest of the nation ardently longs for peace, but without hope of seeing it concluded this soon. Lord Grantham avoids the company of

[25] Formerly ambassador to France and Secretary of State for Foreign Affairs.
[26] The material between the brackets appears only in the photostats.

the foreign ministers in order not to be obliged to answer the questions which they might put to him about the negotiation. I succeeded, nevertheless, in drawing him aside. He told me, apologetically, that his duty, and the nature of affairs, had prevented him, against his wishes, from keeping me informed of the progress of the negotiation, that his present occupations did not permit him to write a long letter to Stepney,[27] but that he begged me to assure Your Majesty that His Britannic Majesty had the same feelings as always toward Your Majesty, that they have already come to an understanding with France on many points of the negotiation, and that according to all appearances they would come to an agreement. I answered him that he had really only confused me with his replies about the progress of the negotiations, and that Your Majesty, being very much interested in the welfare of Great Britain, would be very pleased to learn of the conclusion of the peace. I tried to sound him out on the conditions which were under consideration, but he always eluded my questions.

148: *Nostitz to Frederick II**

MADRID, 6 December 1782

A ship recently arrived at Cadiz from America brings us the news that the English fleet was still in New York in the month of October, only four ships of which were detached to send to Charleston, which are apparently those de la Touche[28] encountered. The English had proposed to General Washington an exchange of fifteen hundred American sailors for fifteen hundred soldiers of the army of Lord Cornwallis, but General Washington

[27] Stepney was the ambassador to Berlin. Shortly Grantham did write a long letter to him which was given to Frederick II.

[28] A French officer taken prisoner by the British. For a letter by La Luzerne to Carleton about his case, see Jared Sparks, *The Diplomatic Correspondence of the American Revolution* (Boston, 1830), XI, 137.

refused this exchange; the American sailors were forced by the British to serve on their ships.

There is some word from London, which is laughed off as untrue here, but which nevertheless is founded on the combinations of English intrigues that Milord Shelburne is carrying on secretly, of designs upon the Spanish possessions on the American mainland. I have seen a letter from London from someone who is in a position to know, who boasts of a project which they have considered, the execution of which would amply compensate England for the loss of her colonies. The forces of England in America consist of forty-six ships and sixteen thousand men, which would indeed appear, with ordinary luck and skill, capable of an undertaking in Mexico, the more so as England does not put much faith in the peaceful intentions of Spain, which nation has no other goal than to ruin the commerce of her rival in America by preventing perhaps one day the entry of cod into this kingdom, and by taking possession of all the commerce of the Gulf of Mexico, especially that of campeachy wood. The Spanish, too long cheated by the other nations, would become, if they had the power, the most intolerable despots in the realm of commerce. It is surprising how many hindrances have been put in the way of what France was doing in this country during the present war, without the latter's appearing, because of politics, to regret it.

149: *Goltz to Frederick II*

PARIS, 6 December 1782

Before we know more here we must, of course, wait a few days for the decision for peace or continued war. That the former is the more probable, I had the honor to write you some time ago; I think I can add, as still another step in that direction, the sending of the son of Count de Vergennes with Rayneval to London, a man probably destined to be the bearer of the preliminaries. As is proper, the greatest secrecy is kept concerning the word sent these days by Rayneval; but as far as I have been able to deduce, it is to say that France, satisfied by the British recognition of American independence, will not insist too much on the cession of one or another conquest made at the expense of the English. According to her principle at the time of the rupture, she saves her dignity by making peace today at this and only at this price. Besides, the ineptitude of Spain in all her operations and the small hope of seeing her improve hereafter, must have been another powerful motive for Versailles to desire peace, as well as the lack of funds; it is certain that this last must have been the same in all the different cabinets. If peace is made, there will be a change in the embassies. Baron Breteuil will be, at last, relieved, as he has been wanting for a long time. I think he will be replaced [in Vienna] by the Marquis de Noailles, former ambassador to London. This choice would give me pleasure. The respectful attachment of all his family to Your Majesty and to the old French policy[29] I do not believe can be doubted. Furthermore, he is devoted to Monsieur, the King's brother, whose principles are not favorable to Austria.

150: *Thulemeier to Frederick II**

THE HAGUE, 7 December 1782

SIRE!

I had committed my very humble report of yesterday, the sixth, to the mails when I was informed that a courier sent posthaste from Paris by the ministers of the Republic had brought the news of the signing of the preliminaries between the Court of London and the United States of America. Another communication of no less importance is that assuring to the Estates

---

[29] Presumably the reference is to the policy of the War of the Austrian Succession when France fought with Prussia against Austria.

General the restitution of the Dutch colonies recaptured by French arms from Great Britain. The latter item is the more reliable of the two because it is certified by a declaration from the Court of Versailles to the ambassador of Holland, in reply to a request of Their High Mightinesses. Furthermore, Brantzen sends word to the ministry of the United Provinces that the main work of the general peace is so well advanced that we are on the eve of the event so consonant with the wishes of all Europe, and that the recognition of American independence by England seems to be announced in a very positive manner. A letter from Count de Aranda to Count de Liano, arrived by the last courier, contains no less certain hopes. The Spanish minister is of the opinion that, if the Court of London carries it to Parliament and has the senate of the nation agree to the unlimited sovereignty of the former British colonies, as it seems to intend, the rapprochement of the belligerent powers will not be long in having the sanction of the ministers holding full powers for that effect.

I have the honor to be, with the most respectful submission,
Sire, Your Majesty's
Most humble and obedient subject and servant,
VON THULEMEIER

151: *Frederick II to Lusi†*

BERLIN, 7 December 1782

From all sides I am informed of apparent circumstances which seem to indicate that the two Courts of Versailles and London are working with an equal zeal for the re-establishment of peace. I am assured that Rayneval has gone to London to call on the British government to recognize, according to their promise, the independence of the colonies, offering for his part to influence the King of Spain to give up Gibraltar and his American conquests. Certain letters from London, under the date of 22 November, announce from another source that the British Court has sent two new emissaries to Paris, Strachey and Roberts, both employed in the departments, and, the latter particularly, in American affairs.   Even from Brussels I have heard that the King of England had postponed the opening of Parliament from 26 November to 6 December, to be able to announce something more definite about the peace treaty; but I admit that I can hardly believe any news of that importance until it is confirmed from your quarter.

152: *Frederick II to Lusi*

POTSDAM, 9 December 1782

I have just received at the same time your reports of the nineteenth, the twenty-second, and the twenty-sixth of November.   I can see by their content that the British government really desires to make peace if it can.   In that it is very right, since it has too many enemies on its hands in the current war, with the result that the sooner it can extricate itself from this situation, without, however, appearing too humiliated, the better.   Regarding what you write me about the English ministers, they do wisely, in my opinion, not to want to make a peace treaty without the participation of Parliament, since if the latter had not agreed first to the conditions, they would surely risk being overthrown, in case the treaty were not in accord with popular opinion.

153: *Goltz to Frederick II*

PARIS, 9 December 1782

But what will be more interesting than these society matters is the course of action the cabinet of Versailles will follow, if in fact, as it now appears, peace with England is concluded soon.

Your Majesty deigns to say that it is very difficult to know what counsel to give to the Turks in this crisis, since by too peaceful counsels one renders them defenseless to their enemies. Your Majesty will already have the goodness to see that Count de Vergennes is also sensible of this difficulty, especially in that he realizes better than anyone how retarded and stripped of resources they are. As since my last interview with him the probability of this eruption in the East has considerably increased, as well as that of an early peace with England, I am not without hope that as a result this minister will be a little more open with me. I think he will be the more willing in that this peace treaty will redound to the credit of Count de Vergennes and restore to him in the mind of his master the power to act according to the true principles of French policy. If I can believe some information from a good source, I will take cognizance of a move which the Court of Vienna made just now. Count Mercy made it known that the Emperor was truly pleased by the progress towards peace among the belligerent powers; but that he did not wish to conceal his astonishment at the refusal of France to the offer of mediation so often reiterated by His Imperial Majesty, that it would have been much more proper to decline it simply at the beginning than now, this monarch finding himself compromised by the offer of his good offices; whether His Most Christian Majesty became displeased at this development by his own course of thought, or whether Count de Vergennes contributed to make him feel so, this much is true, my sources inform me, that the King was wounded by it, finding it highly out of place that such language should be addressed to him. Nevertheless, the reply given to the Austrian ambassador was extremely polite but spoke of the first part of his message, that is to say, of the pleasure the Emperor felt at the progress toward peace. If I may be allowed to express an opinion of this procedure of His Imperial Majesty, he perhaps thought he would constrain them by it at Versailles, and slow down the direct negotiations to make his mediation accepted. From calculating the dates it seems probable that the Emperor instructed his ambassador to do it upon the latter's report that the direct negotiations seemed [not][30] to be succeeding, as was in fact the case, as Your Majesty also will have deigned to see in my very humble reports. As the negotiation suddenly took a turn for the better, the missive arrived here from Vienna at an inauspicious time to have the effect the Emperor hoped of it.

154: *Goltz to Frederick II*

PARIS, 9 December 1782

If the act concluded between the English commissioners and the Americans, of which I gave the abstract to Count Finckenstein[31] in the last mail, were ratified by the English Parliament, I would not be able to recover from my surprise. I do not, in fact, know anything more humiliating than that agreement, especially at the end of a campaign which could be regarded as very favorable to Great Britain. I cannot prevent myself from repeating here a summary which I have from the best source.

Absolute and unconditional independence. The border between America and Canada drawn to the advantage of the Americans. The establishment currently occupied by the English will be evacuated in the term of six months and given over to the Americans.

Newfoundland fishing granted for a certain number of boats.

All the islands within twenty-five leagues distance of the continent of America will be included under the domination of the thirteen states of America. The fate of the Loyalists strongly recommended to the humanity and moderation of the Congress.

[30] In the photostat of the original and in the 1881 copy the words are *"se rapprocher"*, but *"ne rapprocher"* must have been intended, and the sentence has been translated with this correction made.

[31] A cabinet minister of Frederick II.

The sincere desire which those at Versailles have to obtain peace makes them await with great impatience what will have taken place the fifth of this month at the reopening of the British Parliament. The courier bringing the despatches which will announce peace or continued war is expected tonight at midnight or tomorrow morning. I do not dare to hope to be informed of it before closing this very humble report. As to the objects of cession, this is how the negotiation stands now, and how the Bourbon Courts seem to be definitely standing.

The treaty of Paris is taken as the base of the present treaty.

France and England will agree on a full and entire restitution of all that they have captured one from the other.

Gibraltar will be ceded to Spain.

England will obtain in compensation for this establishment, and in way of exchange, Minorca and Guadalupe as well as Florida. France, as indemnity for the generous and voluntary cession of Guadalupe, will be given possession of the Spanish part of the island of Santo Domingo and will occupy the entire island.

East Indian affairs will be reconstituted on the footing on which they stood before the present war, France formally engaging not to erect any fortification or walls or keep any troops in Bengal.

Greater rights to the cutting of campeachy wood in the Bay of Honduras will be accorded to the English than they have enjoyed up to now.

One may with some reason be astonished that in the course of this negotiation there is still no mention of the Dutch or the neutral maritime powers. So the fruit France will garner from the peace, if it be made on the conditions named above, will be the possession of the entire island of Santo Domingo, and to have brought about the dismemberment of America. The last event I know is painful to England, but let us agree also that France is deluded about the advantages she expects to find in it. I see in America, or so it seems to me, only a people poor, exhausted, and afflicted with the vices of the corrupt nations. France and England will carry on there a continual party conflict, both trying to appropriate the principal influence to herself. If one or the other obtains it, according to all humanly discernible probability, it will certainly be England, but the internal divisions which will accompany all that will overthrow the newborn republic and plunge it into final annihilation. When peace is finally signed what will France do? Will she turn, as I see many people are persuaded, to the affairs of the Porte? I do not dare to hope so and even less to believe so, when surveying the exhausted state into which she has fallen. In truth, the King of France's irritation about Count Mercy's explanations on the subject of the small respect for Austrian mediation still persists, but all that will neither last nor have any consequences.

155: *Frederick II to Goltz*

Potsdam, 9 December 1782

In the peace or war question I see that things depend very much on the good propositions that can be made to the English, and on the other hand on the obstinacy of the King of Spain. For the rest, they write to me from Vienna that Baron de Breteuil is getting ready to leave for Paris when the Emperor goes to Pisa. He hopes to obtain a post in the ministry, because the French declare in all quarters that His Most Christian Majesty is dissatisfied with his ministers and wants to put others in their place.

156: *Lusi to Frederick II*

LONDON, 10 December 1782

I have received the gracious instructions of Your Majesty of 26 November by the last express, but that of today brought me nothing from you.

The deliberations of Parliament have not had, these past days, any important matter as their subject; as soon as this assembly takes up any affair which deserves the attention of Your Majesty I will not fail to report it in detail.

It does not yet appear that the negotiation of the peace makes much progress, and no news has come to us from Paris which could raise the hopes of the nation; nevertheless, to judge by the discourse of Lord Grantham, it appears that the British ministry counts on signing the preliminaries of the peace shortly. Rayneval, accompanied by the son of Count de Vergennes, has been seen in public for several days, and the frequent conferences which he is having with Lord Shelburne also prove that on both sides they are serious about negotiating. Meanwhile, the two parties opposed to the ministry, that of Lord North and that of Fox, are active. The latter wants to oppose the cession of Gibraltar and persuade the nation not to consent to it. Its animosity against Lord Shelburne is probably the main motive which drives it to this opposition. Lord North, who wishes no less ill to this ministry, may well on occasion join with the Whigs, a move which could not fail to embarrass the ministry. This party is already quite powerful itself, not only because of the large number of those who compose it, but also because of the eloquence of its chief; but it is said that Lord Shelburne, who does not scruple at the means when he sees an advantage to be gained, is pleased to let the King envisage it as much more dangerous yet than it really is. Under the reign of George I and George II, say the English, the Pretender served as the scarecrow of the House of Hanover, but this menace being out of season, Lord Shelburne

has known how to substitute for it Fox and his party.   The
Count de Kagenek, who arrived here as imperial minister replacing Count de Belgioioso, had a conference with Lord Grantham
in which he renewed the offers of his predecessor of His Imperial
Majesty for the mediation of the peace.   The English minister
replied that when entering upon his present post he had received
a verbal suggestion from the imperial minister, that he had replied
to it then, that the circumstances, not having since changed in
the least, he could add nothing to that reply; that as for the nego-
iation of the peace, he could not conceal from him that the negotiations which were going on at Paris had made some progress,
so that without wishing to reject his offers, he could not accept
them at present, unless all the powers at war who had consented
to negotiate directly should change their minds.   Prince Kaunitz
will be spared the pains to which he wished to go to bring the
belligerent powers to an accord, and we must hope that his intrigues with Russia will succeed no better than his project of
mediation.   Lord Grantham told me that as soon as peace is
made they will undertake the work of concluding the quadruple
alliance which was under consideration last summer, and that
they will soon send someone to St. Petersburg to help Harris[32]
there.

157 : *Frederick II to Lusi*†

BERLIN, 10 December 1782

I have just received, finally, your three despatches of the nineteenth, twenty-second, and twenty-sixth of November, and I see
by their contents that if the British government has for some time
affected little concern for hurrying up the peace making, it has
now, however, changed its tune, and that it has postponed the
opening of Parliament until the fifth of December, publicly announcing to the nation that it hopes to have more assurance either

[32] British ambassador to St. Petersburg.

of peace, or the continuation of the war, by that time. The motives which you attribute to Lord Shelburne appear as well founded as they are probable. It seems, nevertheless, from the frequent sending of secret agents by both sides, and from other circumstances, that the two parties are drawing very close and that they are working with an equal zeal and sincerity for the re-establishment of peace.

158: *Frederick II to Nostitz at Madrid**

POTSDAM, 12 December 1782

I have just received your despatch of 18 November.

Without pausing over your reflections on the re-establishment of the peace, nor on your project of commerce with the American colonies, I am not able, however, to hide from you that this last does not seem to me well reflected. Its execution would necessarily demand a naval force, which I do not have, and our merchant ships would never be able to endure such a long and tiring voyage. Besides, the slightest new war would expose them to the inevitable losses for which there would be no remedy. It would be infinitely better, therefore, that you confine yourself simply to the sole purpose of your mission in Spain, which is to gain favorable treatment for the trade of our Silesian textiles. I have already strongly pointed this out to you several times, and I repeat it to you. That is your task, and you will do well to strive to fulfil it to my satisfaction without distracting yourself with projects for trade which are outside your sphere.

Meanwhile, I have found the last sample of tobacco that I have received from you so exceedingly to my taste that if you could get me twelve livres worth more of it, you would render me a very agreeable service.[33]

[33] Frederick II, a connoisseur of tobacco, seems at this point to be favoring tobacco not from the United States but from the Spanish colonies.

159: *Lusi to Frederick II*

LONDON, 13 December 1782

Lord Grantham told me that the negotiation of peace was well advanced and that he hoped to see peace re-established shortly in an honorable manner.   That is all I could learn from him on this point.

160: *Goltz to Frederick II*

PARIS, 13 December 1782

The King of England's speech, which at last declares the independence of America and the likelihood of an approaching peace treaty, gave great pleasure at Versailles; but in so far as one may see, under the thick veil of secrecy which the negotiations, very properly, maintain, the Court of London, after having taken this great step of recognition, could well be that much stiffer about all the other points, especially Gibraltar.   Perhaps His Catholic Majesty will carry his passion for that place so far as to cede Oran to the English in addition to returning Minorca, and then it would seem that England had made a very good bargain. Florida being kept for Spain, perhaps the latter will relinquish parts of Santo Domingo in favor of France, which will in turn give Guadalupe to England, but meanwhile lose Grenada.   The French would like to have St. Lucia.   In fact, it is of the greatest importance in order for them to look forward to an influence in the Antilles.   Without this station the English would never have been able, in this current war, to maintain themselves in the Antilles with such a decided inferiority in numbers.   I remember often having heard Admiral Rodney say that this station is the most important one for all operations in the Antilles.

161: *Thulemeier to Frederick II**

THE HAGUE, 14 December 1782

The speech given by the King of England at the opening of Parliament having just arrived, I hurry to place this interesting piece before Your Majesty's eyes in a faithful translation,[34] inasmuch as it concerns the recognition of American independence and the negotiation of a peace with the Courts of Madrid and Versailles. I am sending this item for this purpose by way of Hamburg. His Britannic Majesty, in his separate speeches to the House of Lords and the House of Commons, also applauded the arrangements made by the senate of the nation for unrestricted trade with Ireland, gave assurances of his continued desire to effect the strictest economy in the administration of the finances of the realm, and proposed to the Parliament to establish the tranquillity of the vast countries of Asia subject to British rule by means of proper laws.

(Enclosure)

Address of the King of England, given at the opening of Parliament, 5 December 1782[35]

MY LORDS AND GENTLEMEN,

Since the close of the last session, I have employed my whole time in that care and attention which the important and critical conjuncture of public affairs required of me.

I lost no time in giving the necessary orders to prohibit the further prosecution of offensive war upon the continent of North America. Adopting, as my inclination will always lead me to do,

[34] From English to French.

[35] The French translation reported by Thulemeier was a good one. The original version, however, is given here. See *Journals of the House of Commons,* ([London], 1803), XXXIX, 3-5 and *Parliamentary History of England* (printed by T. C. Hansard) (London, 1814). Compare Lusi's report of 6 December 1782, pp. 116-120.

with decision and effect, whatever I collect to be the sense of my parliament and my people, I have pointed all my views and measures as well in Europe as in North America, to an entire and cordial reconciliation with those colonies.

Finding it indispensable to the attainment of this object, I did not hesitate to go to the full length of the powers vested in me, and offered to declare them free and independent states, by an article to be inserted in the treaty of peace. Provisional articles are agreed upon, to take effect whenever terms of peace shall be finally settled with the Court of France.

In thus admitting their separation from the crown of these kingdoms, I have sacrificed every consideration of my own to the wishes and opinion of my people. I make it my humble and earnest prayer to Almighty God, that Great Britain may not feel the evils which might result from so great a dismemberment of the empire; and that America may be free from those calamities which have formerly proved in the mother country how essential monarchy is to the enjoyment of constitutional liberty. Religion —language—interest—affections may, and I hope will yet prove a bond of permanent union between the two countries: to this end neither attention nor disposition, on my part, shall be wanting.

While I have carefully abstained from all offensive operations in America, I have directed my whole force by land and sea against the other powers at war, with as much vigor, as the situation of that force, at the commencement of the campaign, would permit. I trust you feel the advantages resulting from the great branches of our trade. You must have seen with pride and satisfaction the gallant defense of the governor and garrison of Gibraltar; and my fleet, after having effected the object of their destination, offering battle to the combined force of France and Spain on their own coasts; those of my kingdoms have remained at the same time perfectly secure, and your domestic tranquillity uninterrupted. This respectable state, under the blessing of God, I attribute to the entire confidence which subsists between me and my people, and to the readiness which has been shown by my subjects in my city of London, and in other parts of my kingdoms, to stand forth in the general defense. Some proofs have lately been given of public spirit in private men, which would do honor to any age, and any country.

Having manifested to the whole world, by the most lasting examples, the signal spirit and bravery of my people, I conceived it a moment not unbecoming my dignity, and thought it a regard due to the lives and fortunes of such brave and gallant subjects, to show myself ready on my part to embrace fair and honorable terms of accommodation with all the powers at war.

I have the satisfaction to acquaint you, that negotiations to this effect are considerably advanced; the results of which, as soon as they are brought to a conclusion, shall be immediately communicated to you.

I have every reason to hope and believe, that I shall have it in my power, in a very short time, to acquaint you, that they have ended in terms of pacification, which, I trust, you will see just cause to approve. I rely, however, with perfect confidence, in the wisdom of my Parliament, and the spirit of my people, that, if any unforeseen change in the dispositions of the belligerent powers should frustrate my confident expectations, they will approve of the preparations I have thought it advisable to make, and be ready to second the most vigorous efforts in the further prosecution of the war.

162: *Frederick II to Lusi†*

BERLIN, 14 December 1782

The last regular mail not having brought me, to come to the point, any despatch from you, I nevertheless did not want to let today's pass without telling you that according to all the news from Paris the negotiations for peace are progressing in such wise that some think there is already a signed agreement for the American affairs, which becomes at least probable in view of the prompt return of Rayneval to London. It is claimed that what was most repugnant to the King of England was to pronounce the word "independence"; that for this reason the circumlocution has been devised that the King of England will engage to recall his troops from the continent of America, and that independence will be assured to the colonies simply by the guarantee of France. It seems as though all these obscurities ought to be dissipated at the opening of Parliament, which is now taking place.

163: *Frederick II to Lusi*

POTSDAM, 16 December 1782

I can tell you that I have just this moment learned that the peace treaty is made, or at least that the preliminaries are signed, which gives me very great pleasure, because Europe gains by it freedom of commerce, reduction of insurance rates, and public tranquillity.

164: *Goltz to Frederick II*

PARIS, 16 December 1782

We are still waiting here for the latest resolutions of the Cabinet of St. James. The more time drags on, the more fears of seeing the negotiations flounder increase. It is not that the ministry of Versailles has lost all hope of bringing things to a happy reconciliation; nothing could be further from the case; Count de Vergennes has insisted so much to the Court of Madrid, and will insist so much more still, that perhaps it will consent to make some sacrifice for the exchange of Gibraltar, which is the only article now halting the negotiation and holding it in suspense. If I am well informed, England is complaining that the restoration of Minorca has come to be of the smallest importance to her since the Spaniards ruined the fortifications of Fort St. Philip. She still insists on gaining possession of Porto Rico in the Antilles. But the Bourbon Courts hold firmly to their refusal, feeling all the importance of its transfer [to England], since from that moment Santo Domingo and Martinique would lose their value in large measure, finding themselves each under the inspection, so to speak, of Porto Rico. It is to be believed that the belligerent powers, strongly inclined to make peace by their inability to continue the war, will find terms on which they can compromise in this regard. This is something that will be clarified in a few days. The arrival of an English courier, which caused a conference the day before yesterday at Versailles between Count de Vergennes, Count de Aranda, and Fitzherbert, brought nothing conclusive, at least nothing has transpired from it up to the present. The edict of the loan has been registered and published lately. It is very doubtful whether it will find enough credit and confidence to be fully taken up. In short, if anything could make me believe in peace, it is a loan of this description. The capitalists do not find enough inducement to put their money in it, and those who are supplied with even a large number of royal contracts and notes will perhaps be held back by the requirement of paying half in cash.

165 : *Lusi to Frederick II*

LONDON, 17 December 1782

In the midst of the negotiation of peace, the English are making preparations necessary for conducting a vigorous war. As soon as they learned that the French had ordered out of Brest, the tenth of this month, a fleet of ten ships with troops for the islands, they immediately ordered a number of their ships to be held in readiness to depart with four thousand men to reinforce Admiral Pigot, and it is beyond doubt that, if by misfortune the belligerent powers undertake another campaign, the British ministry will be upheld by the nation and will be given all the means to act with force. The wisest part of the nation, in reality, desires peace; but it does not desire it on humiliating terms, and the ministry will be very careful not to accept any terms which are not honorable.

It seems as though the latest letters from Paris have greatly diminished the hopes that were held here of concluding the peace treaty. General Conway told me yesterday that the enemies of England appeared to want to oblige her with another campaign. Meanwhile, the two French emissaries are still here, and are seen everywhere except at the court; but the secrecy is so well kept on both sides that it is impossible to divine what the negotiation is leading to, and which side is making the difficulties. In any case it is certain that the English have concluded and signed an engagement with the Americans under the eyes and with the consent of the Court of France, and based on that fact it seems natural to conclude that this last named court would not have consented to it if it had not been certain of coming to an accord on the other articles, for fear that this commitment, although simply provisional, would determine the Americans not to take part any longer in the offensive against England in case the war continues; and, in fact, it is since the signing of this engagement that people here have begun to predict a favorable outcome for the whole negotiation. They think here that the Spanish claims for Gibraltar and the Dutch demands of restitution of the losses they have suffered will not allow France to conclude a peace treaty very advantageous for herself, but perhaps they are alarmed without cause, and the obstacles that are holding up the negotiations are inevitable but of less importance than they think.

166: *Frederick II to Lusi†*

BERLIN, 17 December 1782

I have received your two despatches of the twenty-ninth of November and the third of December, and I am surprised to find in them still nothing positive about the peace treaty, while Stepney[36] has communicated to my minister a new letter from Secretary of State Townshend in which the British ministry notifies the Bank, or the nation, that the English commissioners have concluded with those of the United States of America, on 30 November, provisional articles which will take effect as soon as the peace between England and France follows. I learn from Paris, at the same time, that the King of England has therein recognized the unlimited independence of America; that he has even stipulated certain terms of friendship and commerce with these states, and that he provides for the interests of the Loyalists rather inadequately. I am assured that the King of England has consented to the cession of Gibraltar, that he has demanded in return Minorca, Florida, and Porto Rico, that the King of Spain still refuses to yield on the last point, but that the ministry of France has undertaken to make him consent to it. If all that is confirmed, the general peace is as good as certain. It remains to be seen how the nation will take the ceding of Gibraltar, especially after the advantages the English gained in the last campaign. As Parliament must be assembled at present, and as the King of England will not have been able to dispense with an explanation to the nation of the terms on which the negotiation of the peace is being worked out, I hope that I will find in your next despatch a detailed and accurate account. The struggles still undecided in

[36] British ambassador to Berlin.

the two Indies can no longer make any difference in the peaceful policy which both sides appear to have adopted.

167: *Lusi to Frederick II*

LONDON, 20 December 1782

The uncertainty in which the public finds itself about the result of the negotiations at Paris gives it hardly any hope of seeing peace concluded and makes most of the nation believe that it will be obliged to continue the war. The ministry, on the other hand, carefully conceals all its proceedings, and the opposition makes an effort to force it to reveal itself in order to cause it embarrassment. Fox and his party, after putting a thousand questions to the ministry about the nature of the treaty concluded with the Americans without receiving the slightest reply, wanted to force them by parliamentary means to communicate to that assembly all the articles which are included, excepting those the publication of which would hinder the negotiations, but principally the articles concerning America and its independence.

The proposition was rejected, and even many of its friends were of the opinion that it could not fail to do harm to the ministry in the negotiations.

168: *Goltz to Frederick II*

PARIS, 20 December 1782

Meanwhile peace seems to become more and more probable since the arrival of an express from London. There was a council [meeting] Sunday, coming out of which the King showed a good deal of gayety, as though he had reason. The negotiators observe the greatest secrecy, but those most able to approach the sources believe they divine the success of the proposal of the

French ministry, to give Gibraltar to Spain, which will give part of Santo Domingo to France, which in turn will cede Guadalupe to England. England leaves to Spain a part of Florida. As for the East Indies, I have sensed in the remarks of someone often consulted about this area by the ministry that things will probably be re-established as they were before the rupture. This man, who knows so much about that part of the world, shudders to see missed the opportunity that they have had for four campaigns to expel the English completely. He does not doubt that the danger, of which they were well aware, will make the English follow more reasonable policies than in the past and develop these possessions to be worth much more than they were formerly to their government and thus to compensate themselves for what they have lost by the dismemberment of America. The slowness of the Emperor's departure from Vienna is wearing out the patience of Baron de Breteuil, who would like to be here more than ever. If peace is made the King will give at least enough of the credit to the Count de Vergennes to permit him to keep his post for a while, but there is talk of a promotion to Marshal of France. The Count [*sic*] de Castries[37] may be the one. That would give him an honorable exit from the ministry, and then Baron de Breteuil could have the Ministry of Marine. As for the Ministry of War, its inadequacy is very well known, and will show up even more when, with the return of peace, they think of rebuilding the land army, completely liquidated in this war. The Marquis of Jaucourt, who has the honor to be known to Your Majesty and who has returned from his expedition to Geneva, could well be given the Ministry of War, the King his master honoring him with his favor. Count de Vergennes is his friend, and he has a good enough reputation in the army.

[37] The Minister of Marine.

169: *Goltz to Frederick II*

PARIS, 23 December 1782

The negotiations with the Court of London seem to tend toward a happy ending.   I had the honor to write you by the last mail of the holding of two councils the same day after the arrival of two expresses from London.   Since then a courier from Madrid, Don Heredia, secretary of the Spanish ambassador here, has left for London.   I suppose he is carrying the ultimatum of His Catholic Majesty and that it is favorable, because a refusal would have been carried by an ordinary courier.   The negotiations have almost escaped from the hands of Fitzherbert; Count de Vergennes undoubtedly preferred to by-pass him and negotiate in London by means of Rayneval, who is entirely his man.   Lord Shelburne himself contributed to this discomfiture for Fitzherbert by sending a number of other emissaries after him.   Among other advantages the Count de Vergennes obtained thereby much greater secrecy than he would have had here from the conferences of all these Englishmen with all the ministers of these different belligerent powers.   Those of Holland are hampered, knowing much less of the details of the actual bargaining than as if the negotiations had been carried on here only with Fitzherbert.   As to the principal conditions of the preliminaries, I can only refer to my former very humble reports.

170: *Frederick II to Lusi*

POTSDAM, 23 December 1782

I have received at the same time your despatches of the sixth and the tenth of this month.   I would strongly hope for the good of Europe that a peace be concluded as soon as possible. I admit that as for the English, it does not appear that they will have reason to press very hard for it, since they have had many

successes this past year and in view of the news which may come
to them yet from the East Indies [*sic*], where in truth the French
have had advantages over them, but where it appears that they
have had their revenge.   I quite understand that they do not yet
want to tell the condition on which they are not yet in accord,
but one can see clearly, in general, how they will go.   In the
meantime I find this accord with the colonies, before the general
peace is signed, a bit precipitate.   I am waiting to hear from you
whether the peace treaty will be made or whether the war will
continue.

171: *Lusi to Frederick II*

LONDON, 24 December 1782

Two Spanish commissioners arrived in London the day before
yesterday, one of whom is Secretary of the Bureau of Foreign
Affairs, and they have taken lodging close to the French commissioners.   Perhaps they are going to smooth out the great difficulty
that the cession of Gibraltar is causing.   It will certainly be decided, on both sides, to make an exchange, but it will not be easy
to come to an agreement about the principle.   It is claimed that
Spain would cede her aquisitions in Florida and the island of
Minorca, and that England demands Porto Rico and Minorca.
This first is very important, the English not being ignorant of
their interests if they demand it, and they would be fortunate if
they received it.

172: *Frederick II to Lusi†*

BERLIN, 24 December 1782

I judge by this address[38] and by what Lord Grantham told
you in general, that the British ministry believes it is quite sure

[38] In the margin appear the words: "which the King of England
delivered at the opening of Parliament."

of peace, and that it is perhaps already in accord with France about the most essential conditions. What confirms me in this opinion is that the King of England stresses so little, in his speech, the efforts to be made for a future campaign, and that he speaks only of domestic affairs in the separate addresses he made to each of the two chambers. As the greater part of the nation is reconciled to the necessity of peace and the condition of the independence of America, it will also approve in the end the ceding of Gibraltar, in return for some suitable equivalent, since it is a place held more for prestige than for necessity. I am, then, expecting to learn soon that the preliminaries have been signed. The opposition party does not appear to be strong enough for, nor even desirous of, preventing the peace, and it will not do anything more than revenge itself for its lack of participation by censuring the conduct of the ministry. If Lord Shelburne keeps to the letter the promise he made to the King his master in his address, he will adopt the essential Whig principles and will thereby carry the vote of the largest party in the country. He will succeed even more if the articles concluded with the United States of America are such that trade between England and America is not hampered and France obtains no advantage.

173 : *Frederick II to Lusi*

BERLIN, 26 December 1782

I am of the persuasion, in reply to your report of the thirteenth of this month, that a peace will be made. The special tax, which I learn the ministry demands, and which ought to run about two hundred million *ecus* [*sic*] for a single campaign, appears to me enormous, and although the nation has stood the war well, especially during this past year, that is not to say that although France and Spain have not given up thinking of Gibraltar these powers will not be in a state to send superior forces to America. For this reason peace suits the English, and, considering the enormous expenses which all the belligerent powers have incurred in general, peace will suit them all equally. I am thus very sure that in about a week or so peace will be signed.

174: *Lusi to Frederick II*

LONDON, 27 December 1782

I have received the gracious *rescrit* of Your Majesty of the fourteenth of December, by which I learn that Stepney announced to Your Majesty's ministry that when the King of England has some expectation of concluding the peace, His Majesty will deem it a pleasure to communicate it to you. Lord Grantham made me the same promise, and that is the sole means by which Your Majesty may be informed of the result of that which is being treated at Paris, for the secrecy about all which pertains to the negotiation of peace is so inviolably guarded that it is impossible to discover the slightest thing, and I have every reason to believe that the British ministry does not want to give any inkling of it to the nation until it is in a position to announce either the rupture of the negotiations or the conclusion of the peace, in order to be able to place before the eyes of the nation in the first case the reasons which will have determined it to prefer to continue the war, and in the second the conditions on which agreement will have been reached for peace. For the rest, if the ministry, against all expectation, should be slow to inform Stepney of the result of the negotiations, I would not, nevertheless, consider it necessary to send a courier to Your Majesty, unless Your Majesty ordered me to do so. The Spanish commissioners whose arrival I mentioned in my last despatch are Don Heredia and d'Agnat. They come from Paris, where they were both in the entourage of the Spanish ambassador.

175 : *Goltz to Frederick II*

PARIS, 27 December 1782

Today I can add the following facts about the peace negotiations. Your Majesty will deign to recall that Count de Vergennes,
despairing of seeing Spain desist from her claim to Gibraltar,
thought of proposing Guadalupe to England in exchange for
Gibraltar and part of Florida, in which case Spain would in
turn cede the Spanish part of the island of Santo Domingo to
France. The Court of Madrid was not very pleased with this
idea, thinking that they would be buying Gibraltar too dearly.
Their ambassador presented his explanation at Versailles with
firmness, and the proposition was changed. Gibraltar no longer
seems to lie so close to the heart of His Catholic Majesty; he
insists upon the cession of Minorca and the rest of Florida, but
does not wish to cede the rest of Santo Domingo to France, which
then no longer would be expected to cede Guadalupe to England.
The Court of London appears adamant against the restitution
of St. Lucia, taken from the French at the outbreak of war, an
island of no commercial importance but of the greatest importance
in time of war because of its port and its favorable position,
giving access to all of the Antilles. As for the East Indies [*sic*],
I am assured that France desires that to the restitution of what
she has lost there in this war be added the Islands of Mahé.
Those would be important to her not only for the various products
but also for the French and Bourbon islands, the Coromandel
Coast, and the Bay of Bengal. I am reminded that the Dutch
plenipotentiaries are anxious, since France is arranging the above
mentioned matters with the English, lest she be less insistent upon
the indemnity sought by the Republic for the establishments
taken at the beginning of the war and upon securing the return
of Trincomalee[39] from the English to the Dutch East India Company. It is sure that should France weaken on this point, her

[39] On the Island of Ceylon.

interests could not help declining in Holland, especially were the Count d'Ademar, who seems destined to succeed the Duke de la Vauguyon[40] if the latter goes to London, to be the one to uphold them, for he, although charming, may very well not get along in Holland because of his hot temper. I may add that while awaiting the final form of the negotiations, the enemies of Count de Vergennes are occupied in raising public opinion against a peace treaty of which they know positively not one word, but which they proclaim to have been foolishly made at a moment when the reinforcement of Cadiz promises, according to them, the conquest of Jamaica, and when the launching of the loan of two hundred million assures the defraying of the cost. The fact is, nevertheless, that at least until now this loan has gone over poorly, and the last levying of the third vingtième suffered the most emphatic reversal in several *parlements,* among others the *parlement* of Besançon.

176: *Frederick II to Lusi†*

BERLIN, 28 December 1782

Your despatch of the thirteenth of December has been delivered to me. It leaves the fate of the peace still undecided. The preparations for war, which are being redoubled in France and England, and the measures taken to find funds for a future campaign, leave no doubt that they are not yet in accord in the negotiations on the essential articles and that they think the continuation of the war possible. Nevertheless, the statements which Lord Grantham continues to make to you and the resolute aspect of the English ministry in the parliamentary debates make me think that the ministry has great hope of arriving this time at the conclusion of a general peace. According to my letters from France the same hope is held there, and it is believed that the

[40] French ambassador to The Hague.

great difficulty will hinge only on the equivalent to be found for the cession of Gibraltar and the objection the King of Spain makes to giving up the island of Porto Rico. If one ought, however, to consider the matter in conformity with the debates of the English Parliament, East Indian affairs would still very much enter into it. It seems, for all this, as though all these uncertainties would end soon and the negotiation of the peace not be long in coming to an end, whether bringing a speedy conclusion or a rupture.

177: *Frederick II to Lusi*

BERLIN, 30 December 1782

My letters from France still speak of an impending peace, and it seems, indeed, in so far as I can judge, that it will yet take place. On the other hand, it is very true that in spite of that the belligerent powers are taking security measures before the peace treaty is confirmed, so that it can very well happen that the respective fleets yet leave port and set sail for America. Perhaps demonstrations of this kind may even speed the negotiations. Time will tell.

178: *Lusi to Frederick II*

LONDON, 31 December 1782

Although there is no inkling as yet of the current state of the peace negotiations, it is spoken of as certain that the government has called off the departure of the reinforcements which it had destined for the islands. The French and Spanish commissioners are still residing here, and couriers come and go continually. One of them arrived yesterday from Paris; but it does not appear that he brought any decisive news. It is very probable that they are already in accord on many points; but there must be many more still to be decided upon. However, provided that the allies sincerely want peace, no difficulties should come from England, where they are convinced that the continuation of the war could not be advantageous to their country. A new loan of twenty million pounds sterling, which will increase the taxes and consequently the price of merchandise, the small probability that there would be of making up this expense by any resulting successes, even the most brilliant, the necessity of bringing back order and economy in its finances, the hope of re-establishing itself in more favorable circumstances, all these conditions will lead England to lend itself readily to the peace, and the ministry, even without its being ruled by the popular opinion of the nation, could not do otherwise than accommodate itself with good grace to the circumstances.

179: *Frederick II to Lusi†*

BERLIN, 31 December 1782

I have received your two despatches of the seventeenth and twentieth of December, by which I see that the British ministry still remains very resolute in the parliamentary debates, and that in spite of all the assaults of the opposition it keeps close censorship over the actual conditions of the peace and over the terms of the negotiations. According to some information which has just reached me, these negotiations are supposed to have taken, all of a sudden, a new turn. England having demanded in return for the cession of Gibraltar the restitution of Minorca and Florida and the cession of Porto Rico and Guadalupe, it is supposed that the King of Spain announced that he wished to withdraw his demand for the cession of Gibraltar, but that he wished to retain Minorca and East Florida, and that a certain Heredia has been sent from Paris to London to present his proposals there. It is generally expected in France that these proposals will be agreed to by England. They tell me that France was already in accord with England, and that affairs and possessions in the East Indies [*sic*] should remain as they were, or ought to have been, according to the last Treaty of Versailles [*sic*]. I wanted to make you a party to this information, for your ears alone, in order that you might follow it up and find out whether it is true, or, if not, on what other terms the negotiation of the peace treaty now finds itself.

180: *Lusi to Frederick II*

LONDON, 3 January 1783

I will not fail to put all my attention on the observations which the direct orders of Your Majesty require and to make every effort to obtain the necessary knowledge in order to make my very humble report on it. But I beg Your Majesty to observe that the state in which Great Britain is going to find herself after the war, as regards her resources as well as the rank she will hold among the other powers of Europe, will depend solely on the conditions under which she will obtain peace and the arrangements that she will make for the administration of her finances and the domestic economy of her domains, and that it is only after these conditions are settled that one will be able to see one's way on the other matters which need time to be compared and digested. The event which will tell us on what footing the English will have been able to settle with their enemies is probably very close; but up to the present one has no feeling of certainty that the preliminaries will be signed. At least that is the way the ministers are talking, and people well versed in these matters are still giving out that there still remain many points to be arranged.

181: *Frederick II to Lusi*

BERLIN, 6 January 1783

People have already wanted to say that the peace negotiations between the belligerent powers have been broken, but I am pleased to see by your report of the twenty-second of December that they are still going on, which makes me believe that they can be finished in spite of all that is said to the contrary. This would not be solely for the good of Europe as a whole, but also to the advantage of England herself. Therefore, as soon as there is any positive sign, be it of the breaking off of the negotiations or of the approaching conclusion of peace, you will take care to inform me. You will be able to let me know all the more quickly by the packet boats, which probably leave more frequently from England for Holland because of the peace negotiations.

182: *Lusi to Frederick II*

LONDON, 7 January 1783

Concerning the settlement which is being negotiated between the belligerent powers, one has not as yet any sure indication which could make one conclude with certainty whether they will agree on the terms, which are still the subject of controversy. Shelburne and the cabinet are still constantly occupied. The French and Spanish commissioners are still here. Couriers come and go, and the negotiations do not seem to be the least bit slowed up, with the effect that if they are acting sincerely on both sides it does not seem doubtful that they will arrive at an agreement; but as the interested parties keep an impenetrable censorship on all their transactions, one cannot judge with certainty what their mutual intentions are, and one is forced to be content here with the speeches of the English ministers, who appear to be persuaded that peace will soon be re-established.

183: *Frederick II to Lusi*†

BERLIN, 7 January 1783

I have received your despatch of the twenty-fourth of December by which I see that the peace negotiations still remain indecisive, or that at least the true circumstances of the situation are kept very secret where you are. According to my information from France and Holland, Spain no longer insists on the cession of Gibraltar and prefers to keep Minorca and Florida. I am assured that the British ministry likes well enough the propositions that the Spanish secretary has brought it, and that it has simply asked for the sending of a negotiator with the necessary powers. Apparently it is in order to have the time to continue this negotiation that Parliament has been prorogued until the twenty-first of January.

They claim, moreover, that the two Courts of England and France have agreed to leave matters in India on the same basis as the Peace of Paris, which appears so much the more likely, because otherwise they would not be so far along toward making the general peace, as all sides seem to recognize.

184: *Frederick II to Lusi*

BERLIN, 9 January 1783

I find exactly nothing in your despatch of the twenty-seventh of December, which I have just received, about what I would like to know—whether it looks more like peace or more like the continuation of the war. You do not say a word about it to me, although that very much interests me at the moment. According to the news that I receive from other sources, it is very apparent that peace will be made, because the King of Spain must have ceased being stubborn on the subject of Gibraltar, which up until now has been the greatest obstacle for the conclusion of the peace, with the result that if that is so, there is every appearance the negotiations undertaken will be able to bring peace because the English have nothing to hope for by continuing the war, except to remain in the terrible situation where they are now; while in making peace they can expect circumstances more auspicious for straightening out their affairs.

185 : *Lusi to Frederick II*

LONDON, 10 January 1783

They claim to know here that the Court of France has demanded a district in the environs of Pondicherry, which would serve to round out that possession and after that the territory of Northern Circars, the Nabob of which is protected by the English. The British ministry, before replying to this demand, wanted to have the opinions of the Directors of the East India Company, who, in the interest of peace, consented to the first of these demands; but the cession of Northern Circars, the sole base which can furnish provisions for Madras, appeared to them very prejudicial to the Company. The British ministry made its reply to the Versailles cabinet in accordance with the advice it had received from the Directors; but the French must have replied that they would not desist from their claim. A council was held on this matter yesterday, but it is not yet known what was resolved. Whatever comes of it, it is hardly probable that France will persist in making such claims. She must fear that the English ministry, which perhaps might not be disinclined to find a pretext to continue the war with her, might come to a settlement with Spain. Moreover, the settlement which has been made with America should make the French consider whether in that case they would find forces strong enough to resist England without the aid of their allies. This concludes, Sire, all that I have the honor to be able to report to Your Majesty today. Whatever weight this news may have, it leads one to believe that in any case they are not yet in agreement in the most important terms of the negotiation.

186: *Frederick II to Lusi*†

BERLIN, 11 January 1783

I have received your despatch of the twenty-seventh of December by which I see that all is quiet in London, and that absolutely nothing is known about the negotiations for peace. According to the intelligence that comes to me from elsewhere, the British ministry indeed agrees to the last proposals of Spain to cede Minorca and Florida and to keep Gibraltar, but she still would like to keep a part of Florida and the Isles of Mahé in the East Indies [*sic*]. It seems, however, that these will not be objects for which there will be general desire to continue the war. Therefore, I am still expecting that peace will come and that we will soon hear of its conclusion, in spite of the preparations that are going on generally.

187: *Frederick II to Lusi*

BERLIN, 13 January 1783

According to all appearances that I see, and according to what you report in your despatch of the thirty-first of December, one may hope that peace will undoubtedly be made. But whether that happens a week sooner or later, it is not necessary to be so exact, and I will be very pleased any time you give me this news.

188: *Goltz to Frederick II*

PARIS, 13 January 1783

As for the negotiations with England, I report an opinion which I think likely, that things are nearly settled with Spain, that is to say by the cession of Minorca and of Gibraltar, that France, not having been able to obtain Dominica, has received Tobago and a share of the fishing of Newfoundland, that besides all will be restored in the Antilles to the situation that existed before the rupture; as for the East Indies [*sic*], the letters of the Count de Suffren,[41] of which I have had the honor recently to speak, having come too late, they did not believe that they should delay the peace for this matter, and they will be content with a few more small factories on the Coast of Coromandel or with the Isles of Mahé. I believe that is the gist of the matter. Count de Vergennes, to whom I have spoken about this only very discreetly, as Your Majesty will deign to believe, told me that while he hoped for the conclusion of peace in a few days, I must realize that it was possible for a negotiation to miscarry at the very moment when it was believed that the treaty would be signed.

189: *Frederick II to Lusi*

BERLIN, 16 January 1783

I doubt, nevertheless, that the negotiations will break down, for, because of internal conditions, the English are in as much need of peace as France and Spain, and I do not see the great hope that exists where you are that one campaign will be able to redress the misfortunes suffered in those preceding. One may be sure that the nation will be greatly weakened after all the efforts it made during this war, and consequently that it will avoid

[41] A French admiral, whose operations supported those of Hyder Ali.

anything which could give rise to new troubles, at least for the next ten years.

190: *Lusi to Frederick II*

LONDON, 17 January 1783

The obstacles which have held up the progress of the peace negotiations until now appear at present to be surmounted, at least for the most part, and although one dare not yet say that peace is certain, nor fix the time when it will be, one is nevertheless generally led to believe that in the course of the next week at the opening of Parliament Lord Shelburne will be in a position to announce to the nation the signing of the preliminaries. The ministry is meanwhile still silent on the conditions of this agreement, and the public knows nothing positive. There is a great deal of talk about it here, and each talker arranges the interests of the belligerent powers to suit himself, so that I believe I would do best to abstain from reporting to Your Majesty vague remarks which would have perhaps no other foundation than the imagination of the speculators of this country, and I will not communicate with Your Majesty until Lord Shelburne offers his explanation at the convening of Parliament, which is to take place the twenty-first of this month.

191: *Grimm[42] to Frederick II*

PARIS, 17 January 1783

The last letter with which Your Majesty honored me was dated from Breslau. The thought of having possibly distracted

[42] Baron Friedrich Melchior von Grimm, born at Ratisbon, an encyclopedist, a friend of Rousseau, had been at the courts of Frederick II and Catherine II. Resident in Paris, he arranged the trip of Prince Henry there in 1784.

Your Majesty a single instant in the midst of your business during such a rapid trip has caused me violent remorse, and I promised myself, Sire, to choose a better time to bring my homage to
the feet of Your Majesty. Carnival time seemed to me the most
favorable. The newspapers tell me, Sire, that you have just
arrived in your capital, followed by the new governor,[43] and my
hands are itching to despatch this letter to greet Your Majesty
returning from the opera or a masked ball. Unfortunately Your
Majesty gives much less time to your amusements than to the
carrying out of your duties of all kinds, and I must hurry indeed.
I risk my letter finding the philosopher, crowned with the diadem
and laurels, already returned to his retreat covered with glory.
However that may be, Sire, you must know that I am preparing
to celebrate the anniversary of the twenty-fourth of January[44]
with the greatest brilliance. Each year adds to the splendor of
this day and confirms the hope that in ten years Your Majesty
will be able to charge yourself with the role of Nestor of glorious
memory by right of age, as you now already enjoy its honors by
the veneration of nations. We here in Paris, naïve and not informed of what is going on, are nonetheless convinced that peace,
the work of Vergennes and Lord Shelburne, is going to be announced right away, in a few days, perhaps a few hours. I never
suspected that on the first trip I should make to Berlin after the
peace I would find a minister of the thirteen United States in-
stalled face to face with the minister of Great Britain, and both
residing near Your Majesty. It is one of those revolutions to
which religion and firm piety teach us to be resolved. Up to
now those of the ambassadors who have not been able to recognize Doctor Benjamin Franklin in his capacity as colleague, have
found in him someone to talk with in the capacity of philosopher;
soon they will be able to deal with him in his capacity of minister

[43] Following the word governor is the clause *"qu'elle vous doit,"* which
does not make sense to the editor.
[44] Frederick II was born 24 January 1712.

of affairs of the two hemispheres, and they will find that they have someone else to reckon with.

192: *Frederick II to Lusi†*

BERLIN, 18 January 1783

I have received your two despatches of the twenty-ninth of December and the third of January by which I see that the hopes of an early conclusion of peace persist in England, without one's knowing, however, anything definite on that score. Opinion is the same in Holland. I know, however, that in France they are beginning to doubt the sincerity of the British ministry and complain of its vacillations. It seems, nevertheless, that on either side they ought to decide soon, if they do not want to remain off guard, and save the necessary time and means still to be able to support the effort of a campaign, if necessary. Perhaps something more positive about it will be learned at the approaching session of Parliament.

193: *Thulemeier to Frederick II**

THE HAGUE, 20 January 1783

The French minister maintains that the peace is very near, and the Grand Pensionary, who enjoys the full confidence of this minister, assured me that the treaty between Great Britain and America was concluded; that not only had the independence of the colonies been recognized, but the limits of the two empires had been laid down; that Spain did not offer any objections which would not easily be met; that as for the peace with the Republic, England would restore Trincomalee[45] and probably ac-

[45] This place on the Island of Ceylon was restored, Great Britain keeping Negapatam on the mainland opposite to Ceylon.

quiesce in the desire of France to see the interests of the Estates General maintained in their entirety.

194: *Goltz to Frederick II*

PARIS, 20 January 1783

Today I can add nothing to my last very humble reports about the peace negotiations, except that the best informed people do not doubt that the signing is very near at hand. In closing this despatch. I am advised that the preliminaries may well have been signed yesterday at Versailles, that the plenipotentiaries have promised to keep the most strict secrecy, in order that it may be declared here and at London, for which city a courier must have left last night.

195: *Goltz to Frederick II*

PARIS, 21 January 1783

SIRE!

The minister of Russia, just now sending a courier for St. Petersburg, has been good enough to include this letter in his packet at the very moment of my return from Versailles. The preliminaries of the peace were signed there yesterday at noon between France, Spain, England, and the United States of America. Holland only signed an armistice, because her plenipotentiaries are still waiting for the authorization to cede Negapatam on the Coromandel Coast to England, a cession without which the Court of London would not consent to restore Trincomalee on the Island of Ceylon. The preliminaries will not be known until the return from London of the courier who left yesterday with the signatures. Fitzherbert held audiences this morning as Minister Plenipotentiary of His Britannic Majesty until the naming of ambassadors respectively.   Count de Moustier leaves for London as Minister Plenipotentiary of His Most Christian Majesty.

I am, &.

196: *Frederick II to Goltz*

(In relation to a despatch of Baron von der Goltz of 21 January.[46]

POTSDAM, 30 January 1783

The news which it contains of the signing of the preliminaries of peace gives me real pleasure.   Great advantage for all of Europe cannot but result from this event.

[46] In the 1881 copies these words in German are at the head of the document.   Since this was placed along with the despatch of 21 January in the 1881 copies, it is here removed from its chronological place in the correspondence.   In the heading Goltz was referred to as *"Graf* Goltz."

Negotiations for the definitive Treaties

In January of 1783 the Dutch would agree only to an armistice, and so the terms of the preliminary treaties did not become final until the Dutch finally signed a treaty, one which was very satisfactory to Great Britain.

Not long after the other preliminaries had been signed, Shelburne, who had salvaged a good deal from a bad situation that had begun to brighten only with Rodney's victory, resigned, to be followed by that combination of opposites, Fox and North. Such parliamentary fickleness as this was beyond Frederick's comprehension. The general unwillingness to engage in further operations worked to the advantage of the British, and by the third of September the Dutch had come to terms, on which date the treaties comprising the Peace of Paris were signed. While keeping Trincomalee on Ceylon, Holland was forced to let Great Britain have Negapatam, just opposite in India, situated favorably for British smuggling. The British in no way recognized neutral shipping rights or paid any damages on this score. What is more, the favorable position of the British in India was heightened by the free trade and navigation rights in the East Indies which the Dutch were forced to grant.

The definitive treaties of Great Britain with France and Spain, although not the treaty with the United States, were signed by Russia and Austria in the capacity of mediators. It was ironic that the French and the British, who so long avoided the proffered actual mediation of the Imperial Courts, should have offered the courtesy of this technicality in consideration of wounded susceptibilities.

Although during 1783 the independence of America had been provided for by the preliminaries, the idea of luring the Americans back was not dead, but neither were the Navigation Acts. While Oswald's successor, Hartley, endeavored to restore something of the old system by promoting the possibilities of trade and defense arrangements, the time for this sort of thing was past, and even the astute Frederick the Great overestimated the possibilities of a collapse of the Confederation and a return of the former colonies.

197: *Frederick II to Lusi†*

BERLIN, 21 January 1783

I have not received any despatches from you in the last two posts, with the result that I am without information as to what is taking place in England regarding the negotiation of peace. According to my letters from Paris of the tenth of January, they think it is now assured and ready to be signed, since an English courier arrived there the sixth and was sent back immediately to London.

198: *Lusi to Frederick II*

LONDON, 24 January 1783

Lord Grantham yesterday evening announced the signing of the preliminaries to the foreign ministers, and he addressed to me the following letter: "By the King's command and for the information of your court, I have the honor to inform you of the arrival of a courier with the preliminary articles of peace between Great Britain and France and between Great Britain and Spain, which were signed at Versailles the twentieth of this month by Fitzherbert and the ministers plenipotentiary of those two courts."

Lord Grantham has just sent a letter to the Lord Mayor of London to announce the same news to him. To this I add that the preliminaries with Holland have not yet been signed, but that they have come to an agreement with this Republic for a cessation of hostilities . . . . [I have just been assured that the main conditions of the peace between France and England are the restitutions of those islands that have been taken except the Island of Tobago, which remains with the French, who will also be allowed to fortify the Islands of St. Pierre and Miquelon. In India Pondicherry will be restored, together with a bit of territory which will round out that possession. The Spanish will keep Minorca and the two Floridas, together with the navigation of the Ohio (*sic*) ;[1] this (right of) navigation has also been granted to the Americans, perhaps expressly to stir up quarrels between the two countries. As for Holland, it is not yet known what agreements will be made, but it is thought that the English do not want to relinquish Trincomalee and that the French will support them in their demands. Well informed persons of that country give assurances that if Holland cedes this possession, as is probable, the English will in a short time persuade the natives of Ceylon to drive the Dutch from that island, and that then the English will be the masters of the commerce of India; this is an eventuality that greatly alarms the powers which hold possessions in this land, especially the Portuguese and the Danes. I am still assured that the English are endeavoring at Paris to make trade treaties with the three powers with whom they have just concluded the preliminaries of peace.]

[1] Mississippi is, of course, meant. Had the plans of Aranda and Rayneval in September succeeded, the Ohio would have been a border. The material between the brackets has been added to this despatch from the photostat of the document.

199: *Frederick II to Lusi†*

BERLIN, 25 January 1783

I have received your two despatches of the sixth and the tenth of January, by which I see that the British government still keeps an impenetrable secrecy on the true state of the negotiations for peace, and it seems to me that the government is even trying to throw the public off the track by all sorts of vague rumors, among which I count what is said about the disagreement which supposedly still exists between the parties over the cessions France is supposed to have demanded in India. According to my news from Paris, which goes up to the thirteenth of January, they are in agreement on the article concerning India; the argument must have centered on the Island of Dominica,[2] instead of which England must have offered the Island of Tobago, which was finally accepted by France, and they expected, at Paris, the return of Count de Vergennes with the preliminaries signed, about the fifteenth of January. One thing which still appears contradictory in the news from various sources is the intention which England just manifested in her public reply to the plenipotentiary of Holland, that they do not want to return to Holland the important establishment of Trincomalee, because the British government must have foreseen that the Court of France would not want to dishonor itself to the point of causing Holland to lose its former possessions. Whatever the result of all these obscurities and uncertainties may be, I do not doubt that they will be dissipated in a large measure by the address the King of England will deliver at the opening of Parliament.

[2] One of the Leeward Islands, between Guadalupe and Martinique.

200: *Frederick II to Lusi*

POTSDAM, 27 January 1783

The peace seems to me now to be assured, but it is also quite natural to presume that after the prodigious efforts which the English have made during this war that they will be obliged to economize for a certain number of years in order to re-establish their resources and their credit, and therefore, at least for ten years after the peace, they will not embroil themselves in any European affair.

201: *Lusi to Frederick II*

LONDON, 28 January 1783

I have received the two latest direct orders from Your Majesty of the ninth and thirteenth of January and your gracious *rescrit* of the eleventh of the same month.

The preliminaries of the peace were presented yesterday to the two chambers. The principal conditions are those I had the honor to report to Your Majesty in my last very humble despatch. I would have liked to be able to send all the details today, but in order to be able to do it with more exactitude I am obliged to put off doing so for the present.

They have not yet signed the preliminaries with Holland here, but they consider that matter as finished, and they expect the ratification at any moment. This peace treaty, which, considering England's situation, ought to be considered the best this country could make, did not, however, very much affect the nation at large, but the public knew that it was a necessity and did not grumble. The same cannot be said for all the members of the cabinet. The Duke of Richmond and Lord Keppel insisted that better conditions could have been obtained. Consequently the former has resigned from the cabinet, although he keeps his position of Grand Master of Artillery, and the other yesterday handed over to the King the Admiralty, of which he was the head. By this time it is easy to see that there will be very important debates in the two chambers, and that the opposition party has become stronger in numbers. That does not mean, in my opinion, that the ministry has not every reason to feel its actions have the approval of the nation, and I think that Lord Shelburne has greatly distinguished himself in this affair, and will be considered a minister who has done much for his country. The debates in the two chambers will give us a better idea of the importance of the cessions made by Great Britain; therefore, I expect to make my very humble report when these discussions are finished, to be able to tell you, Sire, the real truth.

202 : *Frederick II to Lusi†*

BERLIN, 28 January 1783

I see by your despatch of the seventeenth of January that they no longer doubt in London, as they also do not doubt in Paris, the nearness of the signing of the preliminaries of the peace, and that it will be announced to the nation at the opening of Parliament. I expect, then, to receive this news in your next despatch.

203 : *Nostitz to Frederick II**

MADRID, 30 January 1783

I confine myself, Sire, to giving an account of those conditions of this pacification which concern the court where I am resident. Spain keeps Mahon³ and both Floridas, the English Gibraltar and the [privilege of] cutting campeachy wood in the

³ The capital of Minorca, to which island Nostitz was referring.

Bay of Honduras, where, however, the Spanish will establish a commissioner.

This court appears to have bought these advantages cheaply. One reads on their faces, as well as on those of the nation, a marked discontent at not having obtained Gibraltar. The intractable disposition of the ministry still blazes out in an even more unobliging manner for France. There is going to be a tariff, by which French goods are to be treated as badly as possible. In part they are prohibited, in part burdened with duties. In this they treat the English and the Americans with just as little respect.

204: *Goltz to Frederick II*

PARIS, 31 January 1783

Before ending this conversation [with Vergennes], I hintingly inquired of the French minister whether he did not believe that the cession of Negapatam demanded by the English and the consent of France [to it] would strengthen the English party in Holland. Count de Vergennes replied to me that although, indeed, by the expediency of signing the preliminaries promptly the said article might have the suggested effect in Holland, he confided to me, at the time of the negotiation of the definitive treaty France would believe it commensurate with both her dignity and her political interest to look after all points to the advantage of the Republic.

205: *Frederick II to Lusi†*

BERLIN, 1 February 1783

The last mail brought me no despatches from you. However, I do not want to let this mail day pass without writing to you after the great event of the peace preliminaries, signed at Paris, the twentieth of January. You will know of it by now, and also probably the conditions. They are going to be the same ones surmised beforehand, that everything remains on the same footing in Asia, and that Spain renounces Gibraltar and keeps Minorca and Florida. What is new is that England must return the Island of Tobago to France and part of the Banks of Newfoundland, but while returning Trincomalee to Holland, England wishes to take from them Negapatam on the Coast of Coromandel. The plenipotentiaries of Holland, not having authorization for a cession which no one had foreseen, signed only an armistice with England, and they immediately sent their secretary, Tor, to try still to save the town of Negapatam. It seems that the British ministry only insisted on this place of so little importance, which is merely a factory, to mortify and weaken the party which is opposing it in Holland, and it will surely regain the support of the nation if it can change over to the position of returning the place to Holland of its own will. You will try to discover without being too obvious what plan or point of view the English Court had, precisely, in regard to this matter. I believe it will be pleased with what I did for the Prince Stadhouder by the memorandum I sent to the Estates General and by the reply which I addressed to the Estates of the Province of Holland, papers which you will already have found among those published.

206: *Frederick II to Lusi†*

BERLIN, 4 February 1783

I have received your two despatches of the twenty-first and the twenty-fourth of January, from which I learned that the signing of the preliminaries of the peace was then known in London, and that Lord Grantham had told you a great deal about it, but that the conditions of it were not yet entirely known. I learned them from Paris, and I do not doubt that you also know them in detail by now. It is true that this peace is very humiliating for England. She loses not only North America but also the two Floridas, the Island of Tobago, her bases in Africa,[4] half the Newfoundland Banks, Minorca, and her rights in Dunkirk. It is only in the East Indies [*sic*] that England keeps her former advantage and authority. One may guess that a large part of the nation will be unhappy with the peace treaty, and that the opposition will not fail to attack the ministry vigorously, and that a change in administration, but not in policies, may result. I am waiting now until you are in a position to make me more informative and more detailed reports on the reaction and results which this peace produced in England and the measures which the British government will take, not only to re-establish its finances and domestic matters, but to conserve its standing in Europe and participation in foreign affairs.

207 : *Nostitz to Frederick II**

MADRID, 5 February 1783

Spain has not only neglected for a long time to establish advantageous commercial bonds with the United States of America, an opportunity which will no longer present itself, but she still keeps at this moment a profound silence about the recognition of its independence, so that the American minister proposes to force her to do so by threatening to leave.

208 : *Lusi to Frederick II*

LONDON, 7 February 1783

I have received Your Majesty's gracious *rescrit* of the twenty-first of January, and I will not fail to carry it out, at the first op-

[4] Great Britain lost her grip on the Senegal but maintained herself in Gambia.

portunity, the orders contained therein, waiting until the proper time to make my very humble report on the matter. The peace, which has just been concluded, is regarded by the English, who understand the situation in which their country found itself, as the best they could have made under the circumstances. Nevertheless, it does not find universal approbation. The mercantile interests complain of the ruination of their trade, and the partisans of the American Loyalists condemn the ministry for having abandoned people who have lost everything solely because of their attachment to the mother country. The two opposition parties join in this to become an anti-government coalition and to give their objections more weight, holding off only until the moment the preliminaries are examined in Parliament to make their sentiments known. This examination will probably take place in the course of the next week. It is not known that the opposition parties want to contravene the accomplishment of a peace which they desired with at least as much ardor as those who are in power, but their principal object is to overthrow the ministry by condemning the terms to which it consented to subscribe. I do not know to what degree they can expect to succeed, but Lord Shelburne and his colleagues are rather calm about this prospect, and, without trying to seek the support of any party, they are getting ready to put before the nation the methods they employed to execute the orders of Parliament and to obtain peace for England on the best possible terms. As far as the agreement with Holland is concerned, it seems that the British ministry is in no hurry to conclude it and apparently feels certain that the Republic will be obliged to submit to the conditions which the British Ministry offers it with the consent and approbation of France. Lord Grantham is still waiting for the Court of Versailles to reply to the proposition he made concerning the manner of announcing the conclusion of the peace to the supposed mediating powers.

209: *Goltz to Frederick II*

PARIS, 10 February 1783

Your Majesty was waiting for the news, so soon to break, about the peace. You will have had it the next day by my very humble report of the twentieth and will have deigned to see that the conditions are such as I had had the honor to announce in several of my recent despatches. The Republic of Holland has authorized her ministers to agree to the suspension of hostilities but not to the cession of Negapatam. Count de Vergennes recently said to me that she will without doubt still haggle, but that it would be well that this not last for long, because the other powers neither wish nor are able to retard too long the making of the definitive treaty; he impressed on the Dutch ministers that their present assertion of the great importance of this trading post did not correspond with the abandonment in which the East India Company had left it for a long time. Count Heiden fulfilled at Versailles Wednesday the mission he had been given by the Prince of Orange. He came to extend to me his thanks both for the counsel I had given him to prepare for this conference and for the manner in which the Count de Vergennes received him, and which Count Heiden attributed in part, and rightly so, to the interest with which Your Majesty honors the Prince. Count de Vergennes indeed received him in the manner he had promised me. Far from mentioning the refusal of the squadron from Texel and the scene caused at The Hague by the defeat of the French, the minister expressed the confidence felt that in the future the Prince Stadhouder would be more and more persuaded that nothing could be more in his personal interest and the interest of the Republic than to watch over the maintenance of the land and sea forces with the greatest attention; that by this conduct he would gain general esteem and would silence his enemies; that unanimity was indispensable for the well-being of the Republic, of which France was a friend; that France consequently would do nothing to foster dissension, but would always endeavor to foster unity in so far as a foreign power could with decency intervene in internal dissensions. Count de Vergennes closed by saying that the following week he would let him know what the King's orders were; that they would probably contain what he had just said along with the sentiments of His Majesty regarding the gesture the Prince Stadhouder had made in sending Count Heiden. Your Majesty will deign to remember that because of the signature of the letters from the Prince of Orange I was of the opinion I had better not deliver them, and I congratulate myself on that opinion today, since without doubt both the letters and the bearer would have been refused, instead of which I now hope Your Majesty will have reason to be satisfied with the turn this affair has taken.

I see by the above mentioned *rescrit* that the news from Constantinople corresponds entirely to what Count de Vergennes told me of the efforts of the ministers of France and Austria to persuade the Porte to answer Russia's memorandum favorably. But according to my very humble despatch of the seventh of this month, it is only in the first few days of the year that the Porte has given a third reply, perfectly satisfactory to the Tsarina of Russia, and that the French ministry thought it could see the flame being entirely extinguished, or at least the conflagration held off for some time. As to what Your Majesty deigns to tell me of the praise with which you have honored General Elliot and Admiral Howe, I may assure you that, far from causing astonishment here, Your Majesty's greatness of soul in rendering justice to merit wherever found will be recognized here, and if the bulletins received by Your Majesty do not envisage it that way, it is another proof that their editors, as much because they live in a lower class as by default of judgment, know little about the more sensitive segment of society. I may very humbly assure you that these bulletins are so well known here for what they are that hardly any one reads them, and the editors only peddle them in foreign countries. If Your Majesty does not rely on me in this, I dare to beg Your Majesty to ask the opinion of those in whom Your Majesty has complete trust. I beg you, Sire, this favor on bended knee, it being of the utmost importance to me because of the contradiction which can often be found between these sheets and what I have had the honor to write to you. Deign to believe that it is my zeal for the service of Your Majesty which makes me utter this very respectful supplication.

I delivered to Grimm the reply with which Your Majesty honored him.

210: *Frederick II to Lusi†*

BERLIN, 11 February 1783

I have received your two despatches of the twenty-fourth and the twenty-eighth of January, by which I see the country was not very much upset over the loss it has just suffered by the peace concluded at Paris. We must see what will happen in the course of this Parliament, and whether there will be a strong opposition. It seems to me that, after the loss of America, which could no longer be avoided, the most substantial loss England suffers is the competition of the French and the Americans for the fish of Newfoundland, but she gained, or saved, much in keeping her superiority in Asia, where she had everything to lose in the next campaign. Try to find out whether the United States of America has made any treaty with France which gives the French any exclusive trade advantage.

211: *Frederick II to Lusi*

POTSDAM, 13 February 1783

It is a great blessing for the northern part of Europe that the conclusion of the peace has finally been determined.

212: *Lusi to Frederick II*

LONDON, 14 February 1783

There arrived the eighth of this month a courier from Versailles, who brought the preliminaries, ratified and exchanged the third of February, between France and England. Yesterday evening they received likewise the ratification of the preliminaries signed with the Court of Madrid. The peace being still too recent for it to be possible to make a sound judgment on the condition in which it places Great Britain, either in regard to her finances or to her commerce, I must restrict myself for the present to reporting to Your Majesty the measures which the ministry is taking to bring to a close the work for general peace, and to pointing out to Your Majesty whatever may be of interest regarding the internal affairs of this country.

213: *Frederick II to Lusi*†

BERLIN, 15 February 1783

I have received your despatch of the thirty-first of January, and I was surprised to read there that Lord Grantham still wants to propose to the two Imperial Courts that they should sign the definitive peace treaty as mediators. That ceremony would be very extraordinary and new, and I still doubt whether the two Imperial Courts would want to lend themselves to it after being excluded from the mediation itself . . . .[5] As for the peace between England and Holland, it is surprising that it is not definitively arranged with that of the other belligerent powers, and I am curious to know whether England will again insist on keeping Negapatam. It seems as though the Court of London could well return this unimportant place and thereby acquit itself of

[5] The omission was made in the 1881 copy of the document, which was not reproduced in the photostats.

the reparation which, moreover, in all justice it ought to make to Holland for the losses which England caused her before the rupture. This would be the surest way for England to regain her former influence in Holland.

214: *Lusi to Frederick II*

LONDON, 18 February 1783

England has gone through a war in which she lost possessions which were among the principal sources of her wealth. She is menaced by a large emigration of artisans, who will transfer their productivity to America. She will be obliged this year to raise a sum of ten to twelve million to pay up the arrears of the war. Her national debt has accumulated to such a point that the greatest economy would scarcely suffice to bear up this enormous weight which rests entirely upon the fragile base of public credit. Her commerce, considerably diminished by the loss of the monopoly of American products, has need of tranquillity and encouragement to recover some of its strength. Thus the British ministry will have many things to put in order, many conciliations to make, not only to rehabilitate business in the country, but simply to insure its existence and prevent its total ruin. . . . The two Houses of Parliament assembled yesterday at three o'clock in the afternoon, and did not recess until this morning at seven o'clock. A proposal was made to thank His Majesty for the peace he has concluded with France and her allies, which occasioned the examination of the conditions of that peace. The lower chamber voted disapproval of the treaty, and the House of Lords voted in favor of the ministry. We shall soon see whether this diversity of opinion will occasion any change in the administration, a matter on which I will not fail to make my very humble report by the next post.

215: *Frederick II to Lusi*

POTSDAM, 20 February 1783

I do not yet see at all how the opposition can cry out in protest against the present ministry, which certainly has followed a very wise course in the whole matter of the peace making, as according to your report of the seventh of this month it has the intention of doing. But if the English make a bad peace, it should be attributed to the previous ministry, which set all the affairs of England in disorder.

216: *Lusi to Frederick II*

LONDON, 21 February 1783

I seize the opportunity of the departure of an English courier who is going to St. Petersburg to send Your Majesty the printed copy of the preliminary articles of the peace. The despatches with which this courier is charged, as well as those which have been sent to Vienna by another courier, contain, according to what Lord Grantham told me, the formal communication of peace, happily concluded between the belligerent powers, addressed by the cabinet of London to the two Imperial Courts, and an invitation to the said courts to sign the treaty in the role of mediators, and to give full powers for this purpose to their respective ministers at Paris. Lord Grantham also told me that this invitation was made by common agreement with Spain and France, and that they believed it a necessary response to the anxiety which the two courts had shown to implement an agreement by their mediation. . . . As for the treaty with France, it has been observed that the rights given to France to fish on so vast an expanse of coast will entirely ruin English fishing; that the fortifications of St. Pierre and Miquelon will put under surveillance the navigation of the Gulf of St. Lawrence; that the cession of the Island of Tobago will deprive English manufacturing of cotton, which they so greatly need; that the cession made in Africa will render the drug commerce precarious; that the fortification of Dunkirk will be very detrimental to England in time of war, because France could have a large number of ships there always in readiness; and finally that the permission given to fortify Chandernagore in India will render France so redoubtable in that part of the world that in another war she will be strong enough to drive out the English.

The ministry replied to all these points with a good deal of justice and made it plain that England needed the peace in order not to expose itself to general bankruptcy, and that the circumstances demanded sacrifices, but that it would be wrong to say that the small part[6] of Canada ceded to the Americans would deprive England of the great trade she had with the furriers, since the northern part of that province was the most useful for this trade, and besides the importation of that merchandise did not amount to more than fifty thousand livres[7] sterling per year, while the expenses of government cost England eight hundred thousand livres per year. That the Americans had been permitted to fish off Newfoundland in order to win their friendship, and that it was known that even if they had wanted to prevent them from doing so they would not have been able to.

As for the matter of the Loyalists, the ministry replied that Congress would take care of them, and that if contrary to all expectations it does not do so, England will be in a position to provide for them, which will cost her much less than continuing the war. As for the Islands of St. Pierre and Miquelon, the ministry insists that it is not possible to build important ports there; that the place where the French will fish is the least profitable,

[6] In spite of the term here, *"morceau,"* the reference would seem to be to the entire area between the mountains, the Ohio River, and the Mississippi, which by the Quebec Act of 1774 had been included in the administration of Quebec.

[7] The original words were "livres sterling"; the word "sterling" would suggest the possibility that pounds rather than livres were meant.

not only in the number of fish found there, but in the quality of the cod; that the loss of the cotton Island of Tobago will not destroy manufacturing which was in existence before England possessed that island; that what was said about the precariousness of the drug traffic in Africa had not the least appearance of truth; and that the area ceded on the Senegal River cost England many people and much expenditure without her being able to reclaim the least advantage from it; that the cessions made in India and the permission to fortify Chandernagore were necessary consequences of the warning received from those countries where the English troops had mutinied, not having received their pay for four months, while the Company was in the gravest difficulties to find money; that fortunately this circumstance was unknown at Paris; and finally that the advice of the most experienced naval men was that the port of Dunkirk would not be as dangerous as one had believed in the past. The ministry made known also that the English fleet was composed of ninety-nine ships of the line, but that of France and Spain consisted of one hundred and forty-two ships, besides seventeen thousand men they had all ready to send to the islands. In spite of this defense the majority in the House of Commons was against the ministry, and they inserted a clause in the message of thanks to the King, in which they let it be understood that they were not satisfied with the conduct of the ministers and the abandonment of the Loyalists. In the House of Lords the ministry carried the vote by a margin of only six.

(Same despatch) 22 February 1783

Since Lord Grantham held up the departure of the courier until today in order to know the outcome of the motion which was made yesterday in Parliament, I can have the honor of adding that it was proposed in the Lower House to inform His Majesty that his faithful Commons, taking into consideration the relative situation of the contracting parties, find that the concessions made by the ministers cannot be justified. This motion, which was passed by a majority of votes, forces the ministry to quit its posts. I think I will be able even by the next mail to indicate to Your Majesty the names of those who will replace it.

217: *Sandoz-Rollin to Frederick II*

Paris, 21 February 1783

Two days after the discussion about the affairs of Turkey, which I recounted to Your Majesty, Count de Vergennes broached an idea in the council which caused great surprise. It was the idea of requesting the mediation of the two Imperial Courts for the definitive treaty of peace, and of fixing upon a place to hold a congress. The minister read a personal letter from Lord Shelburne, who shares his sentiments and appears to want to conform to whatever France decides in that respect. Two members of the council, Count [*sic*] de Castries and the Marquis d'Ossun, rose to object to the proposal. They represented that, the preliminaries having been signed and all the difficulties being overcome, it was not only useless but imprudent to want to make these two powers intervene in the negotiations. Count de Vergennes upheld his opinion by reasons which prevailed. They consisted principally of the fact that this step was a pure formality and precaution; that since the Court of Vienna has taken offense from the fact that its offers had been eluded, it was not at all unimportant to dissipate its ill-humor; the more so that there must be a proviso in the definitive treaty for the freedom of navigation and maritime principles, which would be extremely repugnant to England, and it would be in some measure the task of the said Courts to fix them in an irrevocable manner for the future. Two couriers were despatched on the eighteenth after this council, one for St. Petersburg and the other for Vienna, bearing this request from France, about all of which the greatest secrecy is maintained. Of all these reasons, as Your Majesty will have had the opportunity to notice, the most pressing was undoubtedly to dissipate the ill-humor of the Court of Vienna about the refusal of its mediation. This is the great object which always occupies the thoughts of Count de Vergennes and which determines the greater part of his actions. If this latest exhibition of feebleness and caution be added to those on which I have already remarked on different occasions, there will be no more doubt, I am sure, of the influence it obviously arrogates to itself in this administration. It now remains to be known whether the two Imperial Courts will take any notice of France for an invitation so uninteresting and useless after the signature of the preliminaries, or whether, on the contrary, their pride will not be wounded by it. That is something I will not delay to ascertain. Then, I still suspect that the influence of the Queen will finally bring her the reins of the government; she seeks to absent the King from Versailles under the pretext that the chateau is falling into ruins, but really to isolate him from the ministers and some of the courtiers, and she will succeed.

I myself hear the Polignac party, which is the dominant party today, reasoning and disposing of intrigue like rulers.

218: *Lord Grantham to Stepney in Berlin†*

ST. JAMES, 22 February 1783

The interest which His Prussian Majesty has taken in the course of our difficult and delicate negotiations, and the desire for their happy conclusion, which His Majesty has repeatedly shown, give us license to make as full communication of this affair as its nature permits in its present state. You may, then, give to the King of Prussia a particular mark of confidence of His [Britannic] Majesty, by explaining to him, for his information, the preliminary articles which have been signed. I will confine myself to saying, as regards the American treaty, that the separation of this country from England having become inevitable, the conditions of the provisional articles are the only ones which could have been obtained, and if it had not been possible to agree upon them, their signing would not have taken place. The speech which the King made at the opening of Parliament so well conformed to this special part of our situation, that nothing can be added to it. Time alone will be able to show the relative situation in which the two lands will be able to exist with regard to each other and prove to what extent this sad separation will be an irreparable calamity for them.

The principles upon which France began these negotiations were very different from those at the end. They indeed offered the Treaty of Paris as the base of the negotiations of the future treaty, but France did not hesitate to ask great modifications and to make it clear that she wished to avoid the restrictions of the Treaty of Paris, which she regarded as humiliating to herself. She will demand explanations and settlements which only the fortunes of war and the state of the acquisitions should permit her to make. The King, wishing to give the most positive proof of his sincere desire for peace, has not insisted on maintaining advantages that the end of the war would let him make, but, consulting only prudence and his attention for the real interests of the realm, has only given resistance to the French demands on points of greater importance. It is thus that the claims of this court in the East and West Indies have been reduced by perseverance to a point which maintains the weight and esteem which Great Britain had before this war.

The coast of the Island of Newfoundland, on which the French are permitted to fish and to dry their catch, is indeed very much wider than that which they had by the Treaty of Utrecht, but on the other hand this fishing is not so rich, their coast was frequented less by our fishermen, and they will be under regulations which can prevent future disputes.

The exceptional development that commerce has made in recent years, and the change that it will probably take since the recent great and new events, have caused France to demand jointly with Spain that some parts of their commercial treaties with this kingdom be revised. Circumstances peculiar to the two states and the opportunity of insisting on new claims which have never been set aside have brought them again under consideration, but this will require a great deal of time and attention to adjust.

The first claims of Spain were exorbitant, their tone as well as their extent. You can easily believe that there was the strongest opposition to them. This kingdom had conquered too large a number of possessions during the course of the war to be able to hope to hold on to all. The retention of Gibraltar renders the loss of Minorca of small meaning, and under the same circumstances there was no need to regret that East Florida was added to West Florida. The right of cutting campeachy wood, established by the Treaty of Paris, has been kept, although it was disputed in the strongest possible manner.

After Holland, having refused the advantageous terms that were offered her for the establishment of the former amity, placed herself among our enemies, France has so strongly supported her claims that it has been impossible to keep the important port of Trincomalee. That objective was looked upon by the Republic with so much jealousy that she would sooner have run the greatest risks than see her exclusive commerce in the Indies endangered by giving up to us this possession, and in this matter she was supported by France, but that court did not hesitate to sign her own articles, since she thought that those that were offered to Holland were of such nature as ought to be accepted for the sake of peace.

Such being the terms of the future peace, it can rightly be said that we have ended a complex and burdensome war, and His Majesty gave way to the most noble sentiments in preferring the re-establishment of the tranquillity of his subjects to the chance of the future successes of his arms.   This development cannot but be most agreeable therefore to the sovereigns who have continued their friendship to the Crown of Great Britain, and there can be no doubt that His Majesty will regard it as fortunate for this kingdom.

One should have thought that the steps toward mediation would have been made in concert by the belligerent powers, but France again took the step of proposing in general to the mediators to decide the negotiations, which could not be refused on our part.   The intervention of these mediators was offered with friendship and accepted with gratitude.   But the circumstances which brought direct overtures for reconciliation between England and France made such rapid progress that there was not time to summon the mediating courts before the signing of the preliminaries.   It can be hoped that their desire to see peace re-established will counterbalance in their minds the degree of personal importance and glory which could have resulted from their intervention, especially if this should have caused the least delay in the conclusion and achievement of the peace.   I hope that they will consider from the correct point of view the progress that has been made in this important affair and those which will still remain to be settled for its conclusion, and that they will want to decline all ulterior intervention, or at least not hinder the definitive treaty by novelties or delays.

219: *Frederick II to Lusi†*

BERLIN, 22 February 1783

I have received your despatch of the seventh of February by which I see that even the peace treaty, disadvantageous as it is for England, is not causing there the agitation and the mass emotion which one would have expected in other times.   We must see what will happen when they debate this matter in Parliament.

220: *Goltz to Frederick II*

Paris, 24 February 1783

The very gracious order of the tenth, with the *rescrit* in cipher dated the eleventh, and another in clear of the tenth of this month on the subject of *non appellando* for the House of Mecklenburg have been safely delivered, and I will immediately obey the instructions contained in the last.

My report of the twenty-first of this month with its post-script is relative to these above-mentioned very gracious orders, not only about the project of the two Imperial Courts against the Turks but about the mission of the Prince of Orange at Versailles. I must content myself today with urgently hoping that Your Majesty is satisfied with the understanding that I give there of Baron de Breteuil's report of the sixth, relative to the above-mentioned project, and of the favorable turn for the Prince Stadhouder which the sending of Count Heiden occasioned. Your Majesty will permit me to report here the substance of my last conversation with Count de Vergennes, which I thought I would not add on the twenty-first, since that despatch was already very long. Being informed from a very good source that the bargain between the Emperor and the Elector Palatine for Bergen-op-Zoom[8] was ready to be concluded, I was not displeased to discover with what point of view Count de Vergennes envisaged this affair. When speaking to me he did not believe it, or pretended not to believe it, so advanced. But at least he admitted to me that if Holland did not pay the Elector all he asked, she would be committing the gravest possible error, since, without a doubt, he agreed with me once the Emperor were master of this place, and consequently of the Scheldt, he would inflict hindrances without end upon the Dutch; he even made me suspect that

[8] A fortified town in North Brabant which joined the United Netherlands in 1576, the hereditary lordship of which remained with the Empire.

realizing their indolence someone had given them the alarm but that their indolence would undoubtedly be as great on this point as on all others. To illustrate it further for me he added that for more than three months he had been asking for their project of peace proposals, in order to combine it with and press it forward with the French negotiation, but in spite of his requests he had never been able to obtain anything but vague replies that they were waiting for the negotiations between the Bourbon Courts and England to take their course; but at last, a few days before the signing of the preliminaries, their ministers had come to bring him, not the project of their final propositions, so long awaited here, but of an agreement for future war operations! His arms fell to his sides with astonishment, and he did not conceal from the ministers that far from making any plan with them for continuing the war, the preliminaries of the peace treaty were going to be signed in a few days. He further told me that now that France had saved them Trincomalee they still continued to hold out against the cession of Negapatam, but that he had told them that however disposed His Most Christian Majesty was to watch over their interests in the peace treaty, he nevertheless would not be too much delayed for that cause, for which reason the Republic would undoubtedly not require France to continue the enormous expenses of a state in arms. If Count de Vergennes wishes ill to the Republic for its repugnance to ceding Negapatam, Brantzen, one of the ministers of the Republic here, confided to me, on his side, the motive for this repugnance. He claims that the chief of the Dutch outposts on the Coast of Coromandel supplies Trincomalee on the Island of Ceylon, and thus, if Negapatam were in the hands of the English, the Dutch possessions on the Island of Ceylon would become precarious. He claims in addition to the foregoing that the English have not failed in their plots to turn the King of Ceylon against the Dutch, and that because the latter overawe him from Negapatam, the moment this port belongs to the English they will stir up the King of the Island to drive out the Dutch. As I made known to Brantzen my astonishment at the fact that for such a long time the importance of Negapatam had not been made known here, since undoubtedly France had fought for this possession as she had for Trincomalee, this minister admitted he himself, along with higher authorities, had learned about this place only a short time ago from a memorandum which the East India Company had delayed much too long in sending. He confided to me that there was a secret negotiation underway by an emissary sent to London, but he agreed with me that not too much could be hoped from it. If the same details have come to Your Majesty by way of The Hague, may I very humbly beg your pardon for having annoyed you with them, but in case they have not I thought Your Majesty would not be displeased to know the present situation of the Republic of Holland relative to the peace negotiations. The favor the King has just accorded to Count de Vergennes does not in truth give him the ostensible influence of Count de Maurepas, but it augments the degree of influence that he had up to now by the need the ministers of the other departments have of the Ministry of Finances. It is believed that Fleury will not want to be subordinated and will ask to resign. The Marquis de Castries, Minister of Marine, always at swords' points with the Count de Vergennes, will scarcely be able to oppose him now that he heads two such essential departments.

His Most Christian Majesty has just conferred on Count de Vergennes the position of Chief of the Council of Finances, which the late Count de Maurepas held, with very considerable emoluments.

221: *Thulemeier to Frederick II**

THE HAGUE, 25 February 1783

Commerce with the American Confederation seems to open
to the Dutch a new field, which appeals to their cupidity. They
have designated for Commissioner General of American Commerce a man of merit, and formerly Director of the East India
Company, while they hasten to exhibit toward the agents of
Congress an obligingness which they can drink in, but of which
a drop in the sale of Virginia leaf tobacco offers a new trial.

222: *Lusi to Frederick II*

LONDON, 25 February 1783

The resignation of the ministry, which I had the honor to
announce to Your Majesty in my last very humble despatch, took
place yesterday. The partisans of Lord North and Fox, who
jointly contributed to this change, will make up the cabinet, replacing those they ousted, but it is not yet known in what way
the posts will be distributed, although it is quite certain that
Fox's party will have the preponderance over that of North in
the administration. This revolution is not making much impression on public opinion otherwise. All that the excitement
of the public amounts to is simple curiosity to know how these
gentlemen of two such different parties will be able to agree on
the division of the posts. I saw Fox yesterday, but being very
busy he had only time to tell me in passing that this change of
cabinet will have no influence on the peace, that it will be scrupu-
lously observed, and that all that has been said to the contrary
was false and counterfeited.

223: *Goltz to Frederick II*

PARIS, 28 February 1783

These same persons [of the inner circle of His Most Christian Majesty whom the Monarch sometimes allows to speak to him of public affairs][9] nevertheless add that since the signing of the preliminaries His Most Christian Majesty was sensible of the political advantage; the glory of that peace treaty appeared to gain in his opinion from the influence that France could have in the general affairs of Europe. Your Majesty will have the goodness to believe that I will leave no stone unturned in instructing myself with the greatest dispatch about the degree of personal attention which His Most Christian Majesty will give to the object in question, until his minister thinks he can offer me further explanation, in case the curtain of this new scene has in fact been raised.

The Bourbon Courts, having constantly refused the mediation of the two Imperial Courts for such a long time and having arrived by negotiating directly with their enemy at a much better peace treaty than they would doubtless have had by the mediators, now think they can make the displeasure caused by these frequent refusals forgotten by inviting the Imperial Courts to appear for the definitive treaty. Two couriers have left for Vienna and St. Petersburg. If the invitation is accepted, it is desired that the negotiations all take place here, and they seem to be determined not to let them be moved elsewhere; but it is predicted that the Emperor, according to his former ideas, will offer Vienna. Undoubtedly the Bourbon Courts have nothing in view but extending courtesy to the two Imperial Courts in calling on them, because by the signing of the preliminaries the basis of the negotiations is well established. Perhaps they hope so to expedite the negotiations with England that when replies come

[9] The words between the brackets are written in the margin of the 1881 copy of this despatch.

from the Imperial Courts, it will only be a matter of obtaining their signatures. I withhold my judgment, but it does not seem possible to me that the guile of the Court of Vienna, interested like Russia in prolonging these negotiations, will permit itself to be a party to this French plan, especially[10] if France has the weakness to remove the negotiations to Vienna. It even seems to me more than probable that the present great commotion in the British ministry will foster this ill-will on the part of the two Imperial Courts against the Bourbon Courts.

224: *Lusi to Frederick II*

LONDON, 7 March 1783

I inquired, conforming to the orders of Your Majesty, whether France had obtained in her treaty[11] any type of trade exclusively; but I was assured that nothing secret existed between those two powers and that the treaty was on the same basis as that which the Dutch have concluded with the Americans.

225: *Frederick II to Lusi*†

BERLIN, 8 March 1783

Your despatch of the twenty-first of February presents me with a picture, as bizarre as it is astonishing, of the situation in which the thoughts and the affairs of the British nation find themselves at present. There are, then, the two parties formerly

[10] The word was *"surtout"* in the original. The writer may have perhaps meant "even if" rather than "especially if."

[11] On 25 February 1783 the United States signed a contract with France, borrowing six million livres at 5 per cent. On 8 October 1782 the United States signed a treaty of amity and commerce with the Netherlands. On 6 February 1778 there had been signed between France and the United States a treaty of amity and commerce.

most opposed to each other, who have joined forces to overthrow the present ministry and to condemn a peace which they themselves rendered necessary, which they demanded not long ago with great outcries, and which the current ministry seems to me to have justified by reasons which are unchallengeable. One would judge by that, that the bulk of the English nation is no longer directed by reason and justice, but solely by the passions of hate, partiality, and private interest. I am very impatient to learn how this affair will be resolved; whether the present ministry will be obliged to yield, and what other will succeed it. If it is composed of a coalition of different parties, it can result only in a malformed and feeble machine, always ready to get itself out of order, and thereby the influence of England in the general affairs of Europe will become insignificant or even non-existent. I have just heard from Paris also the same news which Lord Grantham announced to you, that the Courts of France and Spain have agreed to invite the two Imperial Courts to concur in the final peace treaty as mediating powers. This seems to me singular and disorganized, that three great powers, after concluding the essential part of their peace treaty by the preliminary agreements, go themselves unnecessarily to ask intervention in the final treaty, which is only a formality, by two other powerful courts, and accord them thus a title of guarantee and the right to mix in their private affairs, but I am aware that all this political phenomenon is the result of the weakness which appears as much in the ministry of France as in that of England. Count de Vergennes proposed this invitation of the two Imperial Courts to his own court to please the Queen of France, and the Emperor, her brother, and the British ministry did not dare refuse his proposition, possibly because it also had in mind ingratiating itself by this means with the two Imperial Courts, but before long it will feel embarrassing consequences, since, I know, Count de Vergennes expressly gave as the motive for the proposal, in the French council, that it was necessary to discuss and arrange in concert to obtain in the final treaty articles, which were yet to be put in final form, for maritime neutrality.

As for the peace treaty to be made between Holland and England, I can easily sense from what Lord Grantham told you that the present ministry will not dare to give up any of the conditions involving Holland which France has once accorded to England, however suitable it might otherwise be for England to reconcile herself with the Republic. We will see what the new British ministry will do. If Fox returns to the direction of affairs, he may, following his principles, since he so much disapproved the war against Holland, perhaps draw up conditions for that Republic which she would otherwise have no reason to expect, but this is a subject concerning which only time can enlighten us.

226: *Lusi to Frederick II**

LONDON, 14 March 1783

Meanwhile, his [Lord Bute's] advice will no longer make any difference, since the cabinet will be filled with Whigs, who will limit the influence of the King as much as they can. Several things have already contributed toward diminishing the power of this prince: the cessions made at the peace have not won him the hearts of his subjects; the loss of America has deprived him of an infinite number of positions which he could use as favors for his friends.

227 : *Finckenstein and Hertzberg*[12] *to Frederick II†*

BERLIN, 15 March 1783

The English minister, Stepney, has just read us a despatch from his court in which he is instructed to communicate to Your Majesty the conclusion of the preliminary peace treaties at last, and to explain at the same time the nature and reasons for each stipulation, and to give you to understand that the peace was as good and as honorable for England as the present state of affairs permitted, and that at least she maintained her former weight and luster.   The minister told us that His Britannic Majesty felt that he ought to make this confidential communication to Your Majesty in appreciation of the desire Your Majesty had often evinced for the establishment of peace, and that he might presume Your Majesty would take a friendly interest in this event.   Stepney is told in the despatch that the three courts of France, Spain, and England have just requested again the mediation of the Imperial Courts for the final treaty, but that it was France which made to his chief this proposition which England could not gracefully refuse, and that England hopes nevertheless that the two Imperial Courts will decline a mediation at so late a date, or that at least they will not want to hinder the conclusion of the general peace by injecting new conditions. Such is in brief the communication Stepney made us, concerning which we thought we ought to make our very humble report to Your Majesty.

[Note in the King's own hand.]

Present my compliments and stress my thanks for this communication and say that England has acquired immortal glory by her vigorous resistance to so many enemies, which compen-

[12] Count von Finckenstein and Count Ewald Friedrich von Hertzberg were state and cabinet ministers.   The 1881 copy of this document indicates it was submitted by "Hertzberg-Finkenstein."

sates for some slight losses, for which the wisdom of her government will surely find means to compensate in time.

(signed) FREDERICK[13]

228: *Frederick II to Lusi†*

BERLIN, 15 March 1783

On the order of his court Stepney just brought me a confidential verbal communication of the preliminary articles of the peace and of the motives which guided the British ministry in the course of the negotiation, which resulted in their signature. This overture of confidence, which conforms well enough to details contained in one of your last despatches, while serving to defend the conduct of the English ministers, tends equally to justify the political course followed in this important affair, and to prove that Great Britain has made a peace as honorable as possible for her to obtain in the unfavorable circumstances in which she finds herself. At the same time I was informed of the invitation that the recently belligerent powers have made to the Courts of Vienna and St. Petersburg to intervene as mediators in the definitive treaty, as though it were a step which did not originally come from England at all, but which France had already openly taken before, and to which England was not later able to refuse to accede. I only tell you this for your own private information.

[13] The form in the 1881 copy is "Fédéric," or perhaps "fédéric." The editor of the *Politische Correspondenz* has "Fédéric" at the close of his letters. The signature in the photostats of letters of 1782-1783 is difficult to read.

229 : *Goltz to Frederick II*

PARIS, 28 March 1783

The project of the Court of London of offering great commercial advantages to the United States of America will much embarrass the court here. If England opens all the ports in her colonies to the Americans, France, unless she wishes to displease the latter, cannot refuse to accord them as much in hers, a privilege which will strike a mortal blow at the commerce of the mother country, especially at Bordeaux, Nantes, and Rouen. Besides, they well realize at Versailles, if they do not want to permit the trade competition, the colonies will carry on the trade as contraband, and the Americans will have the same advantage without any gratitude to the French government.

The cabinet of Versailles has not, I believe, taken a stand in this regard as yet, but it is likely that it will resolve upon a middle course, which would be to allow the importation by the Americans of their own products into the French colonies but stipulate that for all other objects whatsoever the importation into these colonies would remain restricted to French shipping. The commercial treaty[14] between Sweden and America, of which I have already had the honor to speak, is going to be signed soon. So far as I could see in conversations with the Ambassador of Sweden, he does not see himself how this commerce could be very lively, the products of the two nations being almost the same, with articles made of copper from Sweden and tobacco from Virginia and the two Carolinas being the only ones which could be made objects of exchange.

[14] A treaty of amity and commerce was signed between the United States and Sweden on 3 April 1783.

230: *Frederick II to Lusi†*

BERLIN, 29 March 1783

This uncertainty [about the English ministry][15] also is delaying without doubt the negotiation of the definitive peace treaty. I am assured that the English ministry absolutely refuses Holland the restoration of Negapatam, as well as the other contested articles, assuring [her] that whatever the new ministry may be, it will never offer better conditions to the Republic, and that the English East India Company has too much influence in England for anyone to be able to sacrifice its interests. Such a tone the British government may successfully use towards a weak power, but by using this tone it will succeed in forfeiting forever a return of close relations.

231: *Frederick II to Goltz*

POTSDAM, 3 April 1783

It is not surprising that France and England have agreed that the two Imperial Courts should sign the treaty of peace, which ought to be concluded, since by means of the preliminaries agreed upon they have already arranged all their differences. These signatures, thus, are only honorary. Meanwhile I know by positive information that the Tsarina of Russia, at the persuasion of the Emperor, is having the translation of a very extensive project of the universal code of navigation for neutrals rushed, with the intention of seizing this moment to propose it and get it accepted by the powers which have been at war. You can inform Count de Vergennes and add that it is believed that these suggestions will be made only for the purpose of halting the definitive conclusion of the peace, with the idea that England would never

[15] The words *"sur le ministère anglais"* appear in the margin of the 1881 copy.

consent to them.   But whatever comes of it, France is very determined to return this mediation to the two Imperial Courts, supposing that these two courts cannot come to an understanding with the Porte.

232: *Goltz to Frederick II*

PARIS, 7 April 1783

Your Majesty will deign to remember that some time ago I had the honor to write of the invitation of the contracting powers, communicating the preliminaries to the two Imperial Courts to accede to the definitive peace treaty.   The Court of Vienna has already replied.   The Emperor is very touched by this obliging invitation and is going to confer at once with the Court of Russia about the proposed intervention.   I do not think I have anything to add to what I have already had the honor to say many times about the regrets the Bourbon Courts may be going to have for having made this invitation.

233: *Frederick II to Goltz*

POTSDAM, 10 April 1783

In regard to world affairs, it is always good that peace be made, for even if France could expect to carry off more advantages in India, she would risk losses somewhere else at the same time. As for the peaceful news Count de Vergennes received from Vienna, I had received almost the same from the same place. But, I do not know why, the news from St. Petersburg is just the contrary.

234: *Goltz to Frederick II*

PARIS, 11 April 1783

I had the honor to write you the seventh that they had received at Versailles the Emperor's acceptance of the definitive treaty. That of Russia has likewise arrived by a despatch of the Marquis de Verac. The ambassador of Vienna and the minister of Russia are awaiting their full powers to sign. The latter will be seconded by Markov, expected from The Hague and going afterwards to Sweden. As Your Majesty predicted, this signing to which the two Imperial Courts have been invited is only a simple courtesy of the contracting powers to make the Imperial Courts forget the constant refusal of their offers of mediation. As the new British ministry is formed at last, the definitive negotiation will not take long to be finally consolidated, since the preliminaries have determined the important points between the House of Bourbon and England. So, in case Holland wants still to hold out against the English demand, I do not think that France will hold up the definitive peace treaty for that reason.

235: *Goltz to Frederick II*

PARIS, 14 April 1783

A courier from The Hague recently brought to the ministers of the Republic the order to insist again, true enough, on the conservation of Negapatam, but in case of refusal to sign the peace just the same if they were obliged to. Your Majesty will deign to remember that Count de Vergennes confessed to me more than once that he did not doubt that England would be obstinate about Negapatam, and that as for the refusal of the Dutch to permit the English free navigation in the Archipelago of the Moluccas, this refusal was unsustainable because contrary to the general freedom of navigation.

236: *Thulemeier to Frederick II**

THE HAGUE, 22 April 1783

The recent connections with the United States of America are taking shape rather slowly. While Adams is still waiting for the ratification of the treaty concluded between the two republics, the departure of the Dutch minister for Philadelphia is held up, and the commerce of the United Provinces with America is not distinguished by any advantages as substantial as had been expected. Although many merchant vessels were sent to Rotterdam, nevertheless up to now it has only been a matter of transporting the products of European manufacture, which Americans will later obtain in their own ships. The financial arrangements with the Republic seem to mean a great deal to the Congress, so much the more so since the need is pressing. But the negotiations undertaken repeatedly and continually at Amsterdam have until now produced but three million florins.

237: *Goltz to Frederick II**

PARIS, 24 April 1783

Markov, minister of Russia, until now resident in Holland and soon to go to Sweden, was expected here yesterday evening, commissioned by the Tsarina to sign the definitive treaty, which is in the offing, conjointly with Prince Bariatinsky, with the accession of their sovereign. Hartley[16] is expected, commissioned, they say, by the Court of London to negotiate a treaty of commerce with the American ministers.

[16] Hartley was Oswald's successor. He worked to re-establish close bonds between Great Britain and America by means of projected trade and defensive agreements.

238: *Frederick II to Goltz*

POTSDAM, 24 April 1783

As regards the peace which will be made with England, I am sure everything will go smoothly, because the English can no longer oppose it now that the preliminaries are signed and that the mediators will not sign except by way of certification.

239: *Goltz to Frederick II**

PARIS, 28 April 1783

I see by the *rescrit* that the arrival of a courier at Stockholm with the commercial treaty concluded here between Sweden and America was announced to Your Majesty. That express may have brought the articles then, ready to be signed but not with the signatures, which did not take place until early this month. Denmark also is occupied in negotiating with America.[17] This treaty may be more essential, not for the Danish products, which are as unlikely items of exchange as those of Sweden for the new republic, but for the Danish islands which could exchange their products.

240: *Goltz to Frederick II*

PARIS, 5 May 1783

As for the definitive peace, it will undoubtedly not take long for it to be signed, as soon as the English ambassador has arrived, but the Dutch are greatly embarrassing the Count de Vergennes. He wants them to sign at the same time as the other powers, while they still firmly refuse to cede Negapatam, a condition without which England does not want to give the Republic

[17] No treaty was concluded.

peace. Count de Vergennes probably does not deceive himself about the fact that if Holland does not accede to the peace treaty, the faction in the Republic favorable to the French will be much diminished, and the Court of London would by renouncing this cession willingly win over the Republic to the terms of the Treaty of 1674.[18] Without, in truth, saying anything like this to me, Count de Vergennes in my last conversation with him nevertheless confided to me again his dissatisfaction with what he called the obstinacy of the Republic. With the preliminaries at hand, he told me, they are disposed entirely against them, because the contracting powers promise to regard as nonexistent any conquests not yet known at the time of signing. But even supposing, as the Dutch very much would like to think, that the Count de Suffren had retaken Negapatam, France would be obliged to return it not to the Republic, but to England. As I am not charged with Dutch affairs, I thought I could dispense with replying, that if he was right in replying thus, the Dutch were not wrong in complaining that the Bourbon Courts having made this accord for their own possessions, as they had the right to do, France was now trying to extend it to apply to the Republic, which had not agreed to these preliminaries.

241: *Thulemeier to Frederick II**

THE HAGUE, 20 May 1783

I hear from a rather good source that according to certain information recently received in Amsterdam from America, the new republic is currently divided into two parties. One, which is not the less numerous, appears disposed to renew relations with the mother country, envisaging commercial bonds established

[18] This treaty had ended the last of the seventeenth-century wars between the English and the Dutch. Its terms had been proposed by Fox in April of 1782. For a discussion and bibliography on this point see Bemis, *Diplomacy of the American Revolution,* pp. 247-248.

with Great Britain as the most suitable, while the other, opposed, regards an alliance with the House of Bourbon as desirable. They assure me that Adams, who was sent with Congressional credentials to Holland, but at the present moment is charged with the negotiation of peace at Paris, has turned coat, and that he has manifested upon more than one occasion remarkable leanings toward England, while his colleague, Doctor Franklin, still perseveres in adhering to his former policy in favor of the Court of Versailles. The commerce between America and Holland, for which such high hopes had been conceived, no longer appears to have the same advantages as formerly, to eyes less predisposed. It is not apparent that luxury would make very rapid progress in a state where the rarity of coinage is making itself felt more and more. It will more likely happen that the low price of manual labor will only aid the Americans, provided moreover with all the most necessary products, to steal from the Dutch a number of branches of trade of which they were in possession until now.

242 : *Frederick II to Thulemeier**

CAMP COERBELITZ, 26 May 1783

I am very much persuaded that this so-called independence of the American colonies will not amount to much, as, it appears by your report of the twentieth of this month, is also envisaged where you are, and that little by little, colony by colony, province by province will rejoin England on their former footing, with perhaps certain advantages which they will stipulate regarding commerce, or other similar matters. I am also very much persuaded that the powers who have been in such a hurry to make commercial treaties with the Americans will not get much advantage from it.

243: *Frederick II to Goltz*

CAMP COERBELITZ, 26 May 1783

Furthermore I would very much like you to talk to Franklin and tell him that there is a great deal of commerce between us and the Americans, which has been carried on for a long time, but which has passed until now through England and through the Dutch; that from our side this trade consisted of fabrics and woolens, and the materials we took from them in exchange were Virginia tobacco, leathers, rice, and sugar; that if Franklin or the colonies wished, we would designate a port of their choice where we could establish this exchange of commerce; that this could be Cadiz, Bordeaux, Nantes, Emden, or Hamburg, as they wish; and that I was obliged to have recourse to this proposition, because, as we have no peace treaty with the Barbary people of Africa, we cannot transport our merchandise all the way to America without too much risk; but that this general proposal that I am making him seems to me the most suitable for both nations; that if Franklin found it acceptable, we could then enter into greater detail and bring these commercial arrangements to their full maturity.

244: *Goltz to Frederick II**

PARIS, 9 June 1783

Following the above acknowledged direct orders, I will speak immediately to the American minister about a trade arrangement to be made with the new republic.

245: *Goltz to Frederick II*

PARIS, 13 June 1783

[I add by postscript to the department of foreign affairs the substance of the commercial treaty between Sweden and America, which I have succeeded in getting for myself.][19] An illness of Franklin has prevented me from making overtures to him about commercial arrangements.

246: *Goltz to Frederick II*

PARIS, 20 June 1783

(Postscript to despatch of this date.)

In consequence of the very gracious order of the twenty-sixth of May, I have made the overture to Franklin relative to the establishment of direct commerce with the Americans. After I told him about the items which the subjects of Your Majesty could exchange for the products of America, he strongly desired an exact and extensive list of them with their price marked in English and in German, which he proposes to send to all the principal commercial houses, from which later Congress will obtain advice for the instructions to give him. He told me first of all, that although the articles of trade produced on the continent were confined to tobacco, rice, and indigo,[20] the Americans could furnish at good prices products of the islands such as sugar and coffee. He added that although he was acquainted with the superiority of the Silesian fabrics, it would be particularly the less fine but also less expensive cloth from Westphalia which would be desired in America; the woolen materials and other

[19] The words between the brackets were added from the photostats.
[20] The cotton gin, which made practical the cultivation of cotton on the North American continent with such significant results, was not invented until 1793.

wool products could make a large item, as also the hardware. Thinking of the part which Polish products might play in this trade, I named to him, among others, wax and honey, but he told me that they did not need them in America. Although he is waiting for the above-mentioned list, he told me that he would inform Congress of my overture at once. As for the depots to be set up in certain European ports, he thinks he can predict that his compatriots would prefer direct commerce, and would come to the ports of Your Majesty's domain, if the consideration of the Barbary pirates, although quite far off the route, prevents Prussian ships from going to America, because of the increase in price that would result from the establishment of agencies, warehouses, and other expenses.

247 : *Frederick II to Goltz*

POTSDAM, 23 June 1783

Fitzherbert, whom you mention, is supposed to pass through here, at which time I may perhaps find the occasion to speak to him. Meanwhile, I am curious to know, when you talked to Franklin, what he replied about our commerce. The proposals which I enjoined you to suggest seem to me to be at least as amenable to the Americans as they are to us.

248 : *Frederick II to Goltz*

POTSDAM, 30 June 1783

I will furnish you with a table of our articles of exchange for the American products, printed in German and English, such as Franklin, according to your postscript of the same date, 20 June

1783, wanted to have to send to the leading commercial houses of the united provinces of the new world, as soon as it is prepared and ready according to the orders I have just given for it.[21]

[21] In spite of this negotiation, the treaty of amity and commerce between Prussia and the United States was not signed by Prussia until 10 September 1785. It was proclaimed 17 May 1786 and ratifications were exchanged 8 August 1786. It was signed by Jefferson at Paris, Franklin at suburban Passy, Adams at London, and Thulemeier at The Hague.

Epilogue

Early in 1783 Frederick the Great had practically assumed that the preliminary treaties of peace would become final. His attention had already turned to problems of peace and to trade in particular. With regard to American affairs he pondered particularly the mercantile problems of a land power prospering in competition with countries possessing empires. In spite of his desire to stimulate Prussian-American trade, however, a treaty with the American Confederation was not ratified by Prussia until 1786. Why was there such a delay? It must be emphasized that Frederick had strong doubts that the Confederation would endure and that he believed the former colonies would drift back one by one into some sort of connection with Great Britain. Furthermore, the French Revolution had not yet occurred. The nature of the republics in Switzerland, Holland, and Venice offered no real threat to monarchical Europe. The aging Frederick quite obviously saw no special threat from republican institutions in America either. In some ways Frederick had a broader view of the War of the American Revolution than the average American today, since he realized clearly that beyond the American commercial and governmental grievances the war was a part of a still broader imperial struggle between the great mercantile powers of Europe. What he did not foresee was that the American Revolution would be permanent and that its ideologies were going to disturb the political order of Europe. In spite of unquestionable astuteness in almost all matters he failed to recognize the ideological significance that went with American independence.

INDEX

Adams, John: negotiations in Amsterdam, 8; approached by British emissary, 18; hears Grenville is stymied, 52; question of peace, 56-57; accused of plot, 70-71; preliminary treaty, 78; visits Franklin, 98; commercial treaty with Holland, 198; said to be pro-British, 201

Africa, Grenville's proposal, 55

d'Agnat, Spanish emissary, 145

Antigua, seizure of, 12 n.

Aranda, Pedro, Count of: proposals for partition of North America, 5; full powers to, 71; opinion on mediators, 92; possibilities of peace, 123; conference of, 137; work with Rayneval, 163 n.

Asgill, British Captain, reported execution of, 63-64

Barbary pirates, influence on Prussian trade, 203-204

Barbé-Marbois, in Philadelphia, 107

Bariatinsky, Prince: Russian ambassador to Paris, 44, 58; with Markov, 198

Bemis, Samuel F., *Diplomacy of the American Revolution* (New York, 1935), cited, 71 n., 85 n., 95 n., 200 n.

Bengal: losses by Holland in, 15; no French fortifications in, 127

Bergen-op-Zoom, 184

Bismarck, Eduard Otto von, German chancellor, reaction to American centennial, xiii

Bouillé, Marquis de: might lead expedition to Jamaica, 49; skill of, 97

Brantzen: Dutch minister to Paris, 71; relations with Fitzherbert, 79; peace negotiations, 123; Trincomalee, 185-186

Breteuil, Baron de: surprised at Kaunitz, 44; new post, 122, 128; eagerness of, 141; report of, 184

de Bussi: operations with Hyder Ali, 48; negotiations with Indian princes, 69-70

Bute, Lord: influence of, 113; system of, 119; diminished influence, 191

Cadiz: objective of Howe, 75; reenforced, 147

Canada, Border of, 126, 177

Cape Clear, objective of Howe, 57

Capellan, Baron, enemy of England, 95-96

Carleton, Sir Guy: peace proposals to Congress, 19, 21; arrival in America, 35; Congress rejects, 47; emissary to New York, 49; evacuation orders, 62; Asgill case, 63 n.

Carolinas: garrisons of, 97; commerce with Sweden, 194

de Castries, French minister of marine: quarrel with Fleury, 86; possible promotion of, 141; opposes congress, 179; relations with Vergennes, 186

Catherine II: interest in the English, 41; advances avoided by France, 53-54; follows Austrian lead, 61; navigation project of, 195

Ceuta, possible exchange for Gibraltar, 33

Ceylon, English policy towards, 163, 185-186

Chandernagore, French right to fortify, 177-178

Charles III: stubbornness over Gibraltar, 60-61; English defense of Gibraltar, 84-85; meeting with d'Estaing, 96; irritated at Vergennes, 104; begged to cede Gibraltar, 109; desires Florida, 115; cession projects, 132; Porto Rico, 139; relents on Gibraltar, 146

Charleston: to be evacuated, 32; proposed cession of, 55; troops taken from, 62, 63; English fleet at, 120

Clarendon, Lord, discussion with Lusi, 14

Clinton, General: peace negotiations with America, 19; arrives from New York, 35

Congress: strength of, 17; British proposals to, 19; trusted by Vergennes, 20-21; possibility of a break with France, 22; will not make peace with England, 24; Vermont's negotiations, 27; possible withdrawal of French minister from, 33; pleased with ministerial change, 35; France concerned about, 40; refuses to treat with Carleton, 47; refuses separate negotiations, 49; avoidance of Carleton, 62; stand on independence, 64; finances, 68; English view of, 70; friendship of Capellan, 96; Loyalists, 177; commerce with the Dutch, 187, 198; to advise Franklin on trade, 203

Conway, General Henry S.: opposes war, 6, 7, 8; defends position, 45; doubts peace near, 138

Cordova, Don, engagement with Howe, 57, 93

Cornwallis, Lord, negotiations concerning exchange of his troops, 120-121

Coromandel Coast: French designs on, 155; Nagapatam, 159, 168

Crimea, role of in Russian diplomacy, 71, 113

Denmark: possible support of England, 34; commercial relations with America, 199

Dominica: taken by British, 79; France not to retain, 155; object of negotiations, 164

de Dorives, French commander in India, 69

Dunkirk: England loses rights in, 169; fortification of, 177-178

Elliot, General, Frederick admires, 100, 172

d'Estaing, Count: strategy of, 75, 85-86; meeting with Charles III, 96; hostile to England, 99; projects of, 102, 104, 114

Evarts, William M., American Secretary of State, letter to American minister in Berlin, xi, xii

Everett, H. Sidney, American minister in Berlin, xiii

Finckenstein, Count: Prussian official, 126; letter of, 192

Fleury, French minister of finances, quarrel with de Castries, 86

Fitzherbert, Alleyne: arrival in Paris, 59, 62; American independence, 64; meets Vergennes, 65-66; role in negotiations, 68-71, 73; relations with Brantzen, 79; renewed activity, 85; quarrel with Vergennes, 99; change in negotiations, 108; conference of, 137; bypassed, 142; role of, 159; signs preliminaries, 162

Florida: Fox willing to cede it to Spain, 23; in preliminary treaty, 77-78; objective of Spanish, 102; Townshend's proposal, 111; sought by Spanish, 115; mistaken report concerning, 127; Spanish possession of, 132, 139, 141; relation to Gibraltar, 143; cession projects, 146, 149, 152, 154; maintained by Spain, 163, 166, 168, 169, 182

Fox, Charles James: favors American independence and other settlements, 23; views on mediation, 25; American independence and peace negotiations, 31-32; attitude on policy, 34; considers mediators, 38; differs with Shelburne, 45; says ministry favors American independence, 48; opposes Shelburne, 50-51, 129; secrecy of ministry, 140; overthrow of ministry, 187; possible policy towards Holland, 191

France: demands American independence, 14, 15, 33, 35; refuses mediation, 29-30; accepts three points of British, 37; continues negotiations with British, 38; concerned about Congress, 40; policy towards Austria and Russia, 41; importance to France of India, 48; utilizes India in negotiations, 52; views of English politics, 58; finances, 68; troops for India, 69; expects fall of Gibraltar, 74; caution toward mediators, 83; desires direct negotiations, 84; tax problems, 88; differences with Spain, 95; problem of the navy, 98-99; colonial rivalry with Holland, 104; Gibraltar, 109; policy changes, 110; financial problems, 137, 147; cession projects of, 146; Northern Circars, 153; doubts English sincerity, 158; signs preliminaries, 159, 161; commerce with America, 194

Franklin, Benjamin: negotiations with Oswald, xiv, 4, 7; relations with Lee and Laurens, 10; approached by British emissary, 18; not suspicious of Vermont, 27; letter to Fox, 32; Grenville to negotiate with, 37; to be assisted by Jay, 40; protests fidelity of Congress, 49; sounded by Oswald, 54; relations with Vaughan, 68; preliminary treaty, 78; Rayneval and conference, 82; visited by

Adams, 98; Grimm's view of, 157-158; still pro-French, 201; role of in Prussian commercial negotiations, 202-205

Frederick the Great, King of Prussia: correspondence with ministers, xi, xii, xiii; desires peace, 3; appreciates Rodney's victory and importance of Gibraltar, 5; views on British policy, 5-6; peace and British politics, 10-11; notes French successes, 12; weighs conflicting interests of the powers, 14-16; British errors, 17; views on continuation of war, 18; doubts British will come to agreement with colonies or Dutch, 22; difficulties of peace-making, 23; surprised at English cabinet, 23; views satisfactory to Fox, 25; surprised at George III, 26; predicts continued war, 36; thinks belligerents should avoid mediation, 42; necessity for American independence, 49; view of conditions, 58; view of Joseph II and English policy, 62-63; expects peace, 76; reaction to preliminary treaty, 79; disgust over Spanish policy, 81; possible mediation of, 86; on state of negotiations, 90-92, 94-95; admires Howe and Elliot, 100; Jamaica, 112; sees signs of peace, 115-116; Prussian policy towards Spain, 131; pleasure over peace, 136; expects peace, 147-148, 151; sees England weakened, 155-156; view of treaties, 161-162; desire for peace, 180; reaction to Grantham's letter, 192-193

Friedlaender, Ernst, Prussian archivist, selection of documents, xiii

Friesland, prepares to recognize American independence, 12

Gallitzin, Prince Dmitri Mihailovich, follows Kaunitz, 44

Gelderland, prepares to recognize American independence, 12

George III: repugnance to American independence, 6; begged to end war, 7; question of the colonies, 8-10; regards Americans as his subjects, 24-25; Frederick II's opinion of, 26; prorogues parliament, 47; necessity for independence, 52; still interested in war, 108; speech of, 116-120, 133-135; reluctance about independence, 136; questions of Porto Rico and American independence, 139; shows peaceful intentions, 144

Georgia: proposed cession of, 55; reported evacuated, 62

Gibraltar: influence on negotiations, 4, 5; wanted by Charles III, 14-15; Fox not willing to cede, 23; possible cession for Ceuta, 33; may be demanded by Spain, 42; Spain's desire for, 47; influence on diplomacy, 58; stubbornness of Charles III, 61; effect on French policy, 62; key consideration, 64-67; British strategy concerning, 71; fall expected by France, 74; defense of, a catastrophe to France, 75-77; Frederick's admiration of the defenders, 78; burning of floating batteries, 84-85; supply of, 87; Frederick's reaction to, 90-91, 93; d'Estaing's mission, 96; Howe supplies, 98; French policy concerning, 109; Count of Artois' tactics, 113; relation to Minorca, 115; Fox's stand on, 119; cession of, 127; Spain's desire for, 132, 138; report England will cede, 139, 141; great problem concerning, 143-144; Spain relents on, 146; relation to Minorca, 148-149; to be ceded, 152; relation to cession projects, 154-155; British retention of, 166, 168; Spanish discomfiture over, 167; Grantham's view of, 182

Goltz, Baron von der, Prussian minister in Paris: correspondence with Frederick II, xiv, 11, 12, 13, 14, 15, 16, 20-24, 26, 27, 33, 34, 35, 36, 37, 38, 39, 40, 41, 42, 43, 44, 47, 48, 49, 50, 51, 53, 54, 56, 57, 58, 59, 60, 64, 65, 66, 69, 70, 73, 74, 75, 76, 81, 82, 83, 84, 85, 86, 89, 92, 93, 95, 98, 99, 100, 101, 103, 104, 106, 107, 109, 110, 113, 114, 115, 121, 122, 124, 125, 126, 127, 128, 132, 136, 137, 140, 141, 142, 146, 147, 154, 155, 159, 160, 167, 171, 172, 173, 174, 175, 176, 177, 178, 179, 184, 185, 186, 188, 189, 194, 195, 196, 197, 198, 199, 200, 202, 203, 204, 205

Grantham, Thomas Robinson, Lord: letter to Stepney, xiv; considered for foreign affairs ministry, 46; arrival of Fitzherbert in Paris, 62; Lusi's view of, 68; vague on triple alliance, 72-73; activities, 80; lack of openness, 87, 99; sounded by Lusi, 105; change in manner, 108; caution of, 119-120; ready for peace, 129-130, 132, 143-144; promise to reveal state of negotiations, 145; statements of, 147; letter to Lord Mayor, 163; waiting for France, 170; proposal to mediators, 174, 176; delays courier, 178; letter on English policy, 180-183

Grasse, Count de: removal of troops from Martinique, 11 n.; advantages of, 16; defeat by Rodney, 34 n., 93; Shelburne's words to, 75

Great Britain: demands return of colonies, 14, 15; burdens of war, 16; thought to be offering favorable terms to America, 18-19; peace overtures to Holland and America, 26-27; avoids mediation, 28; mission of Grenville, 30-31; attempt to detach America from France, 32; to continue American policy and seek a triple alliance, 39; may grant Irish liberties to America, 43; Grenville's proposal, 55; dilatory policy, 80; defense of Gibraltar, 84-85; mediation by Frederick II, 86; empty negotiations, 89; concern over Gibraltar, 94; stiffer attitude, 100-101; renewed efforts, 105-106; financial problems of, 108, 113; King's speech, 116-120, 133-135; Shelburne's projects, 121; ready for peace, 124, 144; commercial and financial problems, 148; weakened, 155; signs preliminaries, 159, 161; Nagapatam, 167; policy towards Holland, 168; politics of opposition parties, 170; Grantham's letter, 180-183; Frederick appraises position of, 173; problems of, at peace, 174; policy explained to Frederick, 180-183; commerce with America, 194

Grenada: Townshend's proposal, 111; cession of, 132

Grenville, Thomas: sent to Paris, 25; mission, 30-34; receives full powers, 35; state of negotiations, 36; three points accepted by France, 37; to broaden negotiations, 37, 40; delays in negotiations, 42; insinuates concessions, 43; question of India and America, 48; recalled to London, 51, 54, 58; lack of success, 52; proposal of, 55; arrival of Fitzherbert, 59

Grimm, Baron Friedrich Melchior von, letter to Frederick II, 156-158, 173

Guadelupe: report of cession, 127, 132, 141; cession projects involving, 146, 149

Haldimand, General, negotiations with Vermont, 27

Harris, Sir James: English minister in Russia, 34, 86; to be aided, 130

Hartley, David: Oswald's successor, 162; commercial relations with America, 198

Hayes, Rutherford B., President of the United States, interest in peace negotiations of 1783, xi

Heiden, Count, mission of, 171-172, 184

Heredia, Don, Spanish emissary, 145, 149

Hertzberg, Count Ewald Friedrick von, letter of, 192

Holland: question of separate peace, 6, 12; competition with England for trade in America, 14; loses in Bengal, 15; Russian relations with, 23; recognition of American independence, 24; refuses peace with England, 26-27; partisans of England, 55; finances, 68; trade treaty with America, 74; colonial rivalry with France, 104, 138; difficulties in negotiations, 142; desires Trincomalee, 146; England to restore Trincomalee, 158; defers signature, 159, 161; Nagapatam, 167; England's policy toward 168; Grantham's views, 182; policy of, 184-186; commerce with America, 187; question of the Moluccas, 197; commerce with America not developing, 201

Honduran coast: Spanish-English rivalry, 102; English rights on, 127, 166-167

Howe, Lord Richard: valor of, 42; may replace Admiral Keppel, 52; question of strategy, 53; success of, 57; future role, 67; tactics at Gibraltar, 75-76; influence of negotiations, 93; feared by French, 95; superiority in ships, 97; supplies Gibraltar, 98; Frederick's view of, 100, 172; possible action in Antilles, 114

Huddy, Captain, Asgill case, cited, 63 n.

Hyder, Ali, operations of in India, 48

India: French successes in, 47; importance to France of, 48, 51-52; Grenville's proposal, 55; role in negotiations, 61, 64-67; French military policy, 69-70; preliminary treaty, 79; Franco-British problem, 80; uncertainty over, 85, 92-93; British success in, 100; King's speech, 118-119; report concerning, 127; future operations in, 143, 148; speculation on, 150; status quo of 1763 to remain, 152; position of England, 161; France to keep Pondicherry, 163; cessions demanded by France, 164; English position, 169; relation to negotiations, 196

Ireland: English troubles with, 13; America and Irish privileges, 43; more liberty for, 46; Newenham, 101; trade with England, 133

Islands of Mahé: French desire for, 146; involved in cession projects, 154-155

Jamaica: invasion not expected, 40; operation canceled, 48; Bouillé might command expedition against, 49; Vaughan, 57; reinforced, 62; Spanish policy concerning, 110; importance to England, 112; French designs on, 147

Jaucourt, Marquis of, possible post for, 141

Jay, John: arrives in Paris, 5; expected to assist Franklin, 40, 49-50; suspicious of Bourbon projects, 77-78; Oswald's commission, 85 n.

Joseph II: seeks triple alliance against England, 34; avoided by England, 36; thought by English less eager, 37; renews mediation offer at Versailles, 39; advances avoided by France, 53-54; pro-French policy, 61; projects of, 92; sensitive about rejection, 125; navigation project, 195

Kagenek, Count de, replaces Belgioioso, 130

Kapp, Friedrich, *Friedrich der Grosse und die Vereinigten Staaten* (Leipzig, 1871), cited, xiii, 39 n.

Keppel, Admiral: may be relieved by Howe, 52; complains about peace terms, 165

Kaunitz, Prince: Franco-Austrian relations, 39-40; initiative of, 43; silence of, 44; awareness of belligerents' avoidance, 54; renewed hopes, 60; leadership of, 61; intrigues of, 130

Lafayette, leaves Brest with troops, 107

La Luzerne: Asgill case, 63 n.; role in America, 107

Laurens, Henry: captured and exchanged for Cornwallis, 10 n.; preliminary treaty, 78

Lee, Arthur, American negotiator in Berlin, 10

Limburg-Stirum, German foreign office official, promises copies of diplomatic correspondence, xii

Loyalists: pitied by Prussia, 3; in preliminary treaties, 77-78; King's speech, 118; fate of, 126; English complaints about, 170; question of Congress, 177-178

Lusi, Count von, Prussian minister in London: correspondence with Frederick II, xiii, 5, 6, 7, 8, 9, 10, 11, 13, 17, 18, 19, 21, 23, 24, 25, 26, 31, 32, 34, 35, 37, 38, 39, 45, 46, 47, 49, 50, 51, 52, 58, 60, 61, 62, 63, 64, 65, 66, 67, 68, 69, 70, 71, 72, 79, 80, 81, 82, 86, 87, 88, 89, 90, 91, 92, 94, 95, 99, 100, 101, 105, 106, 108, 109, 110, 111, 112, 113, 115, 116, 117, 118, 119, 120, 123, 124, 129, 130, 131, 132, 135, 136, 137, 138, 139, 140, 142, 143, 144, 145, 147, 148, 149, 150, 151, 152, 153, 154, 155, 156, 158, 162, 163, 164, 165, 166, 167, 168, 169, 170, 173, 183, 187, 189, 190, 191, 193, 195

Marie Antoinette, relations with Mercy, 60 n.

Martinique: removal of troops from, 11 n.; garrison of, 97; value of, 137

Markov: sent to The Hague, 23; partisan of the English, 27; sent to Sweden, 197-198

Maryland, rejects Carleton, 47

Maurepas, Count de: precipitateness of, 103; influence of, 186

Mecklenburg, House of, 184

Mediation, by Austria and Russia: attempts affecting negotiations, 3, 4; Spain avoids, 16; Frederick thinks belligerents should avoid, 27; French reaction to mediators, 24-26; avoided by Spain, 28-29; France avoids Russian mediation, England Austria's, 36; England might consider, 38; offers renewed, 39; French reaction to, 41; Frederick thinks should be avoided, 42; Austrian initiative, 43; renewed attempts, 53-54; Crimean campaign diverts Russia, 71; France avoids, 73-74; lack of results, 81; French concern over, 83-85; Russian preoccupation in Crimea, 113; Joseph II sensitive, 125, 127; renewed offers, 130; Frederick's view of, 161; Grantham's proposal, 174, 176; proposals for a congress, 179-180; Grantham's views, 183; policy of Bourbon courts, 188-190, 193, 195-196; acceptance of settlements by mediators, 197

Mercy-Argenteau: Austrian ambassador to France, 60; stronger position, 83; reveals attitude of Joseph II, 125, 127

Miller, Hunter, *Treaties and Other International Acts of the United States* (Washington, 1931), cited, 74 n.

Minorca: retention desired by Charles III, 14; capture of Port Mahón, 15; Fox willing to cede it to Spain, 23; Townshend's proposal, 111; connection with Gibraltar, 115; cession of, 127, 132; English complaints concerning, 137; Spanish desire for, 139; related to Gibraltar, 143, 149, 152, 154, 155; Spanish retention of, 168, 169, 182

Mississippi, navigation on, 163

Miquelon: France may fortify, 163; navigation of St. Lawrence, 176; British minimize, 177

Moustier, Count de, leaves for London, 160

Nagapatam: sought by Holland, 159; England obtains, 161; effect on Dutch politics, 167; Holland stubborn over, 171, 185; Frederick wonders about, 174; Vergennes comments on, 197; Dutch hold out for, 199

New England, possible discontent of, 72, 88

Newfoundland: Grenville's proposal, 55; French objective, 65; preliminary treaty, 77-79; Franco-British problem, 80; preliminary treaty, 126; French fishing off, 155, 169; importance of Newfoundland to England, 173; American fishing off, 177; value of French concessions, 181

New York: to be evacuated, 32; rejects Carleton, 47; landing of emissary, 49; reduction of garrison, 50; to be ceded, 55; objective of Pigot, 65; English fleet at, 89, 120

Noailles, Marquis de, new post, 122

North, Lord: fall of ministry, 4; opposition to Conway's motion, 8; difficulties with parliament, 9, 10; appreciated by French, 58; possible return of, 59-60; opposition of, 119, 129; with Fox, 187

Northern Circars, French colonial projects in, 153

Nostitz, Count von, Prussian minister in Madrid: correspondence with Frederick II, xiv, 102, 103, 120, 121, 131, 166, 167, 169

d'Ossun, Marquis, opposes congress, 179

Oswald, Richard: negotiations with Franklin, xiv, 4; new commission, 5; in concert with Grenville, 32; sent to Paris, 54; change of commission, 85, 94

Ouessant, island off Brest, 57

Panin, Count Nikita, former foreign minister, 41

Pennsylvania, rejects Carleton, 47

de la Perouse, French captain, 89

Pigot, Admiral: replaces Rodney, 62; sends ships towards New York, 65, 89; readiness in Antilles, 114; fleet movements, 138

Pitt the Elder, policies emulated by Shelburne, 46

Pitt the Younger, named Chancellor of the Exchequer, 47

Polignac: Duchess de, influence of, 93-94; importance of family, 180

Pondicherry: loss of by France, 14; France demands district near, 153; to be restored to France, 163

Port Mahón: taken by Spain, 15; Spanish retention of, 166

Porto Rico: for Loyalist retreat, 111; English want, 137; relation to Gibraltar, 143, 148, 149

Potemkin, Prince, influence of, 41

Rayneval, Joseph Mathias Gérard de: mission to London, 5; brother of minister to Congress, 71; mission to London, 73, 75, 84-85; with Franklin, 82; departure, 87; second mission, 106-107, 109-110; secrecy of, 121-122; conversations with Shelburne, 129; importance of, 142, 163 n.

Richmond, Duke of: retains post, 45; and American independence,

46; complains about peace terms, 165

Roberts, English emissary, sent to Paris, 124

Rockingham, Charles W., Marquis of: fall of cabinet, 4; compared with Shelburne, 38; relations of Thomas Townshend to, 46; death of, 58

Rodney, George Brydges, Lord: victory in Caribbean, 5; re-enforcement of, 11 n.; victory over de Grasse, 34; replaced, 62; view on St. Lucia, 133

Russia: sends Markov to Holland, 23; possible support of England, 34; concern over Grenville's mission, 38; renews mediation offer at Versailles, 39; following Austrian lead, 43; advances avoided by France, 53-54; Crimean campaign, 71, 106; mediation by, 161; relations with Turkey, 172; policy toward Turkey, 184; accepts settlements, 197

St. Augustine, reported evacuated, 62

St. Christopher: seizure of, 11 n., 12 n.; preliminary treaty, 79

St. Lucia: Rodney's view of, 132; England insists on, 146

St. Pierre: France may fortify, 163; navigation of St. Lawrence, 176; British minimize, 177

Sandoz-Rollin: correspondence with Frederick II, 30, 31, 33, 179-180

Santo Domingo: allies assemble forces in, 49; reports concerning, 127, 132; value of, 137; part to go to France, 141; cession projects, 146

Savannah: to be ceded, 55; reported evacuated, 62, 63

Schulenburg, Baron von, Prussian minister, 103

Shelburne, William P. Fitz-Maurice, Earl of: work admired by Frederick II, xvi; forms cabinet, 4; considered for prime minister,

7; appointment to cabinet, 13; compared with Rockingham, 38; policy compared with Fox's, 45-47, 50-51; sends Oswald to Paris, 54; Vaughan, 57; precarious position, 58; French mistrust of, 66; confidence in Fitzherbert, 68; views on American independence, 72; message to de Grasse, 75; the preliminary treaty, 77-79; with Grantham, 80; question of American independence, 107; still interested in war, 108; extends negotiations, 111, 113; system approved, 119; projects of, 121; conversations with Rayneval, 129; motives of, 131; bypasses Fitzherbert, 142; possible success of, 144; busy with negotiations, 151; announcement awaited, 156; work with Vergennes, 157; praised, 166; tactics of, 170; backs Vergennes on congress, 179

Simolin, Russian ambassador, role of, 18, 70

Spain: wants Gibraltar and to keep Minorca, 14; takes Port Mahón, 15; avoids mediators, 28-29; may demand Gibraltar, 42; expects reduction of Gibraltar, 52; financial resources of, 56; stubbornness of king, 60-61, 81; English defense of Gibraltar, 84-85; money not available in Holland, 88; goals in America, 102-103; policy changes, 110; goals of, 121; cession possibilities, 132; pressure for Gibraltar, 138; signs preliminaries, 159, 161; discomfiture over Gibraltar, 167; commercial relations with America, 169; Grantham's views on Spanish policy, 182

Sparks, Jared, *The Diplomatic Correspondence of the Revolution* (Boston, 1829-1830), cited, 63-64 n., 120 n.

Stadhouder: activities of Adams towards, 70-71; Capellan opposes, 95-96; Frederick's relations with,

168; future policy of, 171; position of, 184

Stepney, British minister in Berlin: instructions from Grantham, xiv; not yet instructed by Grantham, 120; transmits information to Prussia, 139; state of negotiations, 145; Grantham's letter, 192, 193

Steuben, General von, descendants invited to Yorktown centennial, xiii

Stormont, Lord, opposition of, 119

Strachey, English emissary, sent to Paris, 124

Suffren, Count de, French admiral, 155, 200

Thulemeier, Prussian minister at The Hague: correspondence with Frederick II, xiv, 52, 53, 55, 56, 57, 68, 70, 71, 72, 74, 88, 95, 96, 98, 105, 122, 123, 133, 134, 135, 158, 159, 187, 198, 200, 201

Tobago: preliminary treaty, 79; France to receive, 155, 163, 164, 168, 169, 176, 178

de la Touche, French naval officer, involved in prisoner exchange, 120-121

Townshend, Thomas: replaces Shelburne, 46; letter of, 110, 139; indication of peace, 116

Trincomalee: desired by Dutch, 146, 158, 159; reported gained by Dutch, 161; England's attitude on, 163, 164, 182, 185

Vaughan: negotiations of, 57; relations with Franklin, 68

Vaudreuil, French naval commander: heads for Chesapeake, 65; success of, 89

Vauguyon, Duke de la: question of formal Franco-Dutch alliance, 27; possible replacement by Count d'Ademar, 147

Vergennes, Count de: informed of Frederick II's views, 15; doubts America will negotiate separately, 20-22, 24; conference with Grenville, 31-32; caution towards mediators, 39-40; aware of English politics, 52; avoids mediators, 53-54; Grenville's proposal to, 55; view of North, 58; reaction to English politics, 59-60; receives Fitzherbert, 62, 65-66; Asgill case, 63 n.; avoids English negotiations, 73; naval policy, 75; handling of mediators, 83-84, 92; distress of, 93; quarrel with Fitzherbert, 99-100; dilemma of, 104, 107; Russian projects, 113; Rayneval's mission, 114, 121-122; policy towards Turks, 125; pressure on Madrid, 136-137; position of, 141; bypasses Fitzherbert, 142; problems facing, 146-147; work with Shelburne, 157; expected back, 164; promises support for Holland, 167; relations with Dutch, 171-172; proposes a congress, 179-180; relations with Dutch, 184-185, 191; position of, 186; invitation to mediators, 190-191; navigation project of Russia, 195; view on Nagapatam, 197, 199

Vermond, Abbé de, relations with Marie Antoinette, 60 n.

Vermont, negotiations with British, 27

Virginia: rejects Carleton, 47; commerce with Sweden, 194; role of in Frederick's commercial scheme, 202

Washington, George: Prussian view of, 19; Asgill case, 63; exchange of prisoners, 120-121

Wharton, Francis, *Revolutionary Diplomatic Correspondence of the United States* (Washington, 1889), cited, 63-64 n.

White, Andrew D., American minister to Germany: informed of Prussian correspondence, xii

William I, German Emperor, interest in American centennial, xiii

Yorke, General, aids Grantham, 80

Yorktown: centennial of, xiii; negotiations following, 3